Brownells Guide to
101 GUN GADGETS

Useful Tools and Accessories
Every Shooter Must Own

COMPILED AND EDITED BY
TODD WOODARD

Skyhorse Publishing

Skyhorse Publishing books may be purchased in bulk at special discounts for sales promotion, corporate gifts, fund-raising, or educational purposes. Special editions can also be created to specifications. For details, contact the Special Sales Department, Skyhorse Publishing, 307 West 36th Street, 11th Floor, New York, NY 10018 or info@skyhorsepublishing.com.

Skyhorse® and Skyhorse Publishing® are registered trademarks of Skyhorse Publishing, Inc.®, a Delaware corporation.

Visit our website at www.skyhorsepublishing.com.

Library of Congress Cataloging-in-Publication Data is available on file.

10 9 8 7 6 5 4 3 2 1

Library of Congress Cataloging-in-Publication Data is available on file.

ISBN: 978-1-62873-677-9
E-book ISBN: 978-1-62914-110-7

Printed in China

Got comments, corrections, or conversations? "Like" the Brownells page on Facebook, or email the author at wtoddwoodard@gmail.com.

Note: Every effort has been made to record specifications and descriptions of guns and ammunition accurately, but the Publisher can take no responsibility for errors or omissions. Also, Publisher advises that prices for items may change, or items may be discontinued, and the Publisher can take no responsibility for those errors or omissions.

CONTENTS

INTRODUCTION

I remember the moment the idea for this book hit me. I was writing video scripts for Brownells in 2011, and as the result of the research necessary to do that freelance work, I was waist-deep in specifications and descriptions of hundreds of products. Script after script I kept saying to myself, "I had no idea such a thing existed." Then I came across this item: The Remington 700 AICS Stock by Accuracy International.

I've shot a lot of 700s over the years, but I've never owned one. The mere existence of the AI chassis made me want to rush down to my primary testing facility, Tactical Firearms in Katy, Texas, and buy a 700 off the wall. Because, as I eventually wrote,

> "Accuracy International's fully assembled tactical-stock chassis converts a Remington Model 700 barreled action into a versatile sniper rifle, with no specialized gunsmithing or stock bedding needed. Simply drop a Model 700 barreled action into the Accuracy International Chassis System, or AICS, and secure the action with two bolts. The self-aligning, self-bedding aluminum 'V' block chassis allows the barrel to float for superior accuracy. The chassis is molded into a fiberglass-reinforced polymer stock that won't flex or warp, regardless of changes in temperature or humidity."

I'm sorry, that's just a cool item. Then I realized that I had seen dozens of cool items for rifles, pistols, shotguns, cleaning, sights, slings, holsters, and everything else in the Brownells catalog and on the websites for its associated companies, The Police Store and Sinclair International.

As the editor of *Gun Tests* magazine, I like to think I'm reasonably well informed about most gun things, but at that time, I didn't schedule many accessories tests. So I checked my reader mail and saw repeated requests for information about accessories—chronographs, toolkits, optics, slings, and a ton of other items we never touched because the test schedule was full of guns. But one reader pointed out that he likely had purchased all the guns he would ever own, but he was extremely interested in tinkering with them and upgrading them, and he had the money to do that.

That convinced me to contact Jay Cassell, Editorial Director for Skyhorse Publishing, about doing an accessories book. I sent him a list of 527 video scripts I had written for Brownells, and told him that didn't even scratch the surface of what Brownells stocked. There were tens of thousands of SKUs, I said, and some genuinely interesting and helpful products were waiting, like buried treasure, to be found.

Jay and I met with Pete Brownell in Las Vegas, and in short order, Pete agreed to let the project go forward with the company's cooperation, and on the spot he came up with five or six other follow-on ideas based on his comprehensive knowledge of the company's vast range of products.

The issue, then, became a matter of judgment about what to exclude. When you're editing from a list of so many products, you're bound to leave out something that someone would have found useful. I leaned heavily on the good nature of Larry Weeks, Brownells' head of press relations and a longtime employee, and Lawrence Hansen, the lead copy- and technical writer for the mammoth annual Brownells catalog, to help me winnow and organize the choices.

I have handled nearly all the products in this book and have purchased many of them. In some cases, I've interviewed folks who had a product of interest and who were willing to share their experiences with me. I am not a gunsmith, so the complexity of the products I've chosen as cool gadgets reflects the immediate utility it can provide the shooter. Many items snap or bolt on your firearms; many items make the snapping and bolting on of other products easier. The items are described, in general terms, by how I use them. Their "gadget number" precedes the name of the product, and the Brownells code follows the name of the product, so when you log on to Brownells.com or peruse the catalog, you can find it.

If you own or use a product that you think other shooters should know about, contact me at wtoddwoodard@gmail.com and let me know. After compiling these hundred-odd gadgets, that only leaves about 19,900 others to go, and I'd love to know what you think are gadgets you can't do without.

Todd Woodard
Houston, Texas
July 20, 2013

CHAPTER 1

BASIC GADGETS

Tools are like experience—you accumulate them as you need them. But there are a handful of tools every shooter should own just to make life easier.

A good way to start is with **#1 Brownells' Basic Gunsmith Kit (080-750-000, $293)**. Gunsmiths, avid hobbyists, armorers, and all manner of shooters run into many of the same cleaning, disassembly, and maintenance problems. One way to amass the tools you need to solve these problems is to encounter a glitch, and get the tool to fix it. Or you can invest in a collection of specialized tools whenever you can lay your hands on them.

Practically all professional gunsmiths own the twenty-four tools (plus six additional screwdriver bits) in this kit and use some of them every day. I've grown to know the true value of this kit because good friends who are starting to work on guns ask me for tools out of it all the time. When they ask for a particular tool the second time, I still loan it out, but I suggest they invest in the tool themselves. Also, this is my primary go-to-the-range box because of its versatility.

Of the items in the kit, I personally use the hollow-ground screwdriver bits and Magna-Tip handle the most. I've written about the Magna-Tip handle in great detail elsewhere, but it's worth mentioning a couple of things about the #81 Handle. For most work, I prefer the #81's solid handle better than the #84's hollow handle. Also, I prefer the longer shank on the #81 because I often want light directly on the work surface and a little more working distance makes that easier. The #81 also includes a powerful magnet that transfers magnetism through the bit, which holds screws in place. On the bits themselves, the long taper of the "hollow-ground" blades transfers the force over the whole screwdriver tip, reducing stripping.

The two smaller instrument screwdrivers are for sight work. The larger one works well on Marble, Redfield, Williams, and other sights that may need

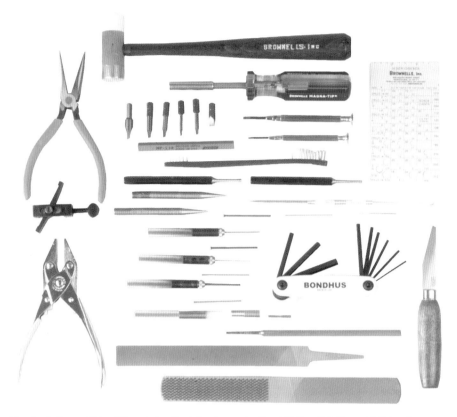

The Basic Gunsmithing Kit contains the following tools: No. 100 Parallel Pliers; 1" Nylon/Brass Hammer; No. 81 MAGNA-TIP® Screwdriver; Screwdriver Bits Nos. 1, 2, 6, 00, 10, 20, and 30; Two sizes Instrument Screwdrivers; Main Spring Vise; MF134 India Stone; M-16 Brush; ⅛" x 6" Pin Punch; 5⁄32" x 6" Pin Punch; 1⁄16" Starter Punch; 3⁄32" Starter Punch; Brownells Replacement Pin-Punch Set; 2" Replacement Punch Assortment; Nylon/Brass Drift Pin Punch Set; Gunsmith Bench Knife; 8" No. 2 Cut Hand File; Sight Base File; 4-in-1 Hand Rasp; Scribe-Hook; No. 1033 6" Chain Nose Pliers; No. 91 Allen Wrench Set; Screw Check'r and Kit Box.

blade adjustment. The small one will work on smaller front pistol sights and very small rear sight screws.

I also use the cleaning brush a lot. Like you, I've used worn-out toothbrushes for cleaning, but this one is better. It was developed for the US Armed Forces to clean M16/M4 rifles quickly and effectively. The double-ended, solvent-proof, polypropylene handle provides a large, contoured series of nylon bristles to cover curves and open areas. The short, extra-stiff, narrow line of bristles tackles tougher crud in hard-to-reach areas. I've used mine to get down inside actions, pistol slides, on black powder guns, and around the extractor star on revolver cylinders, to name a few areas. Solvents such as d'Solve, EZ-Soak, WD-40, and Hoppe's bore cleaners haven't phased it.

The Allen-Wrench Set is handy and versatile, and a surprising number of guns these days have Allen heads. I change handgun grips a lot, and I prefer the look and functionality of an Allen-head screw in replacement panels.

There are two starter punches included: a ¹⁄₁₆ inch and a ³⁄₃₂ inch. They can break loose a stuck pin better than a long drift punch or pin punch. There are two larger 6-inch pin punches, one ⅛ inch and one ⁵⁄₃₂ inch for heavier jobs. Also in the kit is a Nylon/Brass Drift Punch Set. The replaceable tip has both brass and nylon fittings. The brass head is excellent for many jobs, but when it is used on blued surfaces, it is possible to get brass marks on the metal. But by using the nylon tip (which has a steel insert to keep it from breaking), you can drive out a front sight or a pin without marring or transferring brass coloration to the finish. These are all used with a Brass/Nylon Hammer as the situation demands.

Five more tools in this kit get steady use as well.

The Chain-Nose Pliers are stout but still grip small things like pins and springs well. The pliers are also the right length to reach in on many guns and squeeze the link connecting the action spring follower and action bar assembly together for removal.

The Scribe Hook works great for marking a line on something with a pointed instrument, aligning pins in holes, pulling springs into place, and getting inside tight places and jiggling things.

The Sight Base File is a three-square file with two safe sides. I use it for fitting front or rear sights, and making inserts for front sights.

The Mainspring Vise doesn't see heavy use but is handy when working on sideplate shotguns or muzzleloaders by controlling the mainspring.

Parallel Pliers aren't made for the usual twisting/turning jobs; rather, their parallel jaws grab springs and rounded objects without them slipping out between the jaws when you apply pressure. Tip: Use a heavy rubber band and wrap it twice around the grips to make a useful small vise.

Three material-removal tools help make specialized jobs simple and easy. The 8-inch Hand File cuts metal beautifully and has one cutting edge and one safe edge. The 4-In-One Hand Rasp removes wood quickly and in a variety of shapes and cuts. The India Stone is a basic, all-around hone.

Rounding out the kit are three items that see occasional use. The first is a Screw Check'r gauge. When you have to replace screws, it saves a lot of time because it lets you know what size to order or replace. For shaping, inletting, incising, and relieving, the Gunsmith Bench Knife is a favorite of wood and leather workers. And the Replacement Pin Punch Set has industrial "piercing punches" made to withstand a lot of stress. If they get bent or broken, they're easy to replace in the special handle.

The **#2 Assembly/Disassembly Mat (358-128-316, $23)** is such an unremarkable, basic product that you must wonder what it's doing in this collection—its function is just to lay there. That's precisely why it's an overlooked gun gadget all shooters should own.

In its most basic formulation, a bench pad is insurance. At some point, you'll lay your 1911 slide on the kitchen table for just a sec (because that's where the best light in the house is), gouging a dent in a wood surface or dinging a glass top, or you'll scrape a piece off your gun's finish on a metal lip. The non-shooting spouse in the house is unhappy about the first one; the shooting spouse is unhappy about the second one.

Obviously, when working on any firearm, the surface you are working on should be clean, smooth, and free of any material that will scratch or mar the finish. Some gunnies like to lie out a whitish towel for their disassembly/reassembly work, which makes some sense. Parts don't go everywhere, the gun is protected, and they can see dark metal items.

The downsides are obvious. Small parts pick up lint; fluids seep through the fabric, and a vital screw can embed in the fluff and wind up falling to the ground unnoticed.

The surface of the Assembly/Disassembly Mat is hard enough to keep dirt and bits of metal from embedding, solvents and oil won't pour through, and it's tough enough to stand some abuse.

Because of those characteristics, there are lots of ways to use these mats in "unapproved" ways. They're flexible enough to be rolled up for storage, and soft enough to lay or sit on. I keep a clean(ish) small mat (17 ½ inches long, 12 inches wide, and ³⁄₁₆ inches thick) in my car toolbox and have used it as a floorboard mud guard, sat on it doubled up on aluminum football stands, spread it out at the range to keep small tools from rolling off a benchtop, and once used it rolled up as a pillow. The large mat (36 inches long, 24 inches wide, and ⅛ inch thick) makes a passable upper-body prone mat for shooting in dirt.

The Brownells Assembly/Disassembly Mats should be cleaned periodically with warm water and detergent to remove any oil, grease, or dirt from its surface. The Assembly/Disassembly Mats are resistant to most solvents and oils commonly used with firearms. *Photo courtesy of Levergun4570sbl from Fairfield, California.*

All that utility from something that just lays there.

The **#3 Gun Cradle by Mountain Meadow Woodworks (612-001-000)** has been discontinued by the maker, unfortunately. That's a shame, because it served as a rock-solid helper for a variety of gunroom tasks. With a firearm fixed in the Cradle, I had both hands free to make short work of cleaning, bore-sighting, installing scopes or sights, or even applying Acraglas for bedding jobs.

What I liked about the Cradle was its simplicity. I placed a rifle or shotgun into the Cradle and secured it with a wooden clamp. Leather pads in the front V-support and under the pistol grip protected fine stock finishes. Also,

The discontinued Gun Cradle was made of oak veneer and hardwood and measured 27 inches long, 8 inches wide, and 7 ¾ inches tall. It's worth keeping an eye out for a used one in a gunshop or in auctions, like GunAuction.com. Also, if you're handy with wood, you can examine the photos and get a good idea about how to rough one out and get the same utility.

the eight-pound Cradle had non-skid rubber feet so it didn't slide around. A base-tray lip kept small screws and other parts from rolling away.

A smaller alternative to the Gun Cradle is the **#4 MTM Portable Maintenance Center (574-101-000WB, $48)**, which comes in a Portable and Gunsmith's style. I prefer the Gunsmith's version, which is 29 ½ inches long, 9 ½ inches wide, and 4 inches high.

Made of polypropylene, the Maintenance Center holds rifles and shotguns in padded forks for cleaning and minor gunsmithing. Use it to mount scopes and swivels.

If you want to step up a grade, the **#5 Battenfeld Technologies Best Gun Vise by Tipton (100-012-229WB, $130)** works with nearly all rifles, shotguns, muzzleloaders, AR platforms, and pistols. It is fully adjustable to accommodate nearly all lengths of firearms. A rubberized cradle and jaws protect and grip the guns while a quick-release cam action allows for easy access. Molded-in compartments hold solvents and small parts and are made of tough, solvent-resistant polymers. All contact points are coated with non-marring surfaces.

A central aluminum channel lets the user move individual components to the ideal position for each firearm. Each individual component then adjusts to the perfect position for secure support. The rear base features two

The #5 Battenfeld Technologies Best Gun Vise by Tipton is fully adjustable to accommodate nearly all lengths of firearms. A rubberized cradle and jaws protect and grip the guns while a quick-release cam action allows for easy access. *Photos courtesy of Battenfeld Technologies.*

The Best Gun Vise's three supports are adjustable for positioning on the base via the T-track, and they all offer vertical adjustment. The rear clamp blocks can accommodate practically any stock configuration, style and size of cheekpiece, or cast-off.

adjustable offset clamps for a tight grip on a range of buttstock configurations.

The Best Gun Vise's three supports are adjustable for positioning on the base via the T-track, and they all offer vertical adjustment. The rear clamp

The rear clamp base features two vertically independent adjustable clamp blocks.

base features two vertically independent adjustable clamp blocks, each with a padded jaw that can be positioned at different points from the centerline. With this flexibility, the rear clamp blocks can accommodate practically any stock configuration, style and size of cheekpiece, or cast-off.

For cleaning most long guns, including bolt-actions, it makes sense that the muzzle of the barrel be lower than the breech to prevent solvents, oils, and other liquids from running back into the breech area. To do this, maneuver the stock and/or the rear clamp base so that the pad contacts the stock at different points, either raising or lowering the height of the rear of the rifle. Then, the forend support can be raised or lowered to achieve the desired elevation. A variety of pistols and revolvers can be held in the Best Gun Vise by turning the rear clamp support 180 degrees and using the vertically adjustable clamps to hold the handgun by the grips. Then position the barrel on either the grip support or the forend support.

The next two items could just as easily be called specialized AR-15 tools and appear in a later chapter, and by their functions, of course they are suited just for ARs. But so many people own AR variants these days, these tools have become basic items to start with, in my opinion. If you don't own an AR yet, then skip over these two.

The **#6 and #7 AR-15/M16 Action Block/Lower Receiver Vise Block Set (080-000-659WB, $80)** eliminates the use of a specialized barrel vise when removing or replacing the barrel assembly on AR-15/M16 rifles. The heavy-duty Action Blocks and insert allow you to firmly clamp A1, A2, and

The solvent-resistant structural Rynite Action Block and insert surround the entire upper receiver and support it inside and out to make rebarreling the AR-15/M16 an easy, one-man job.

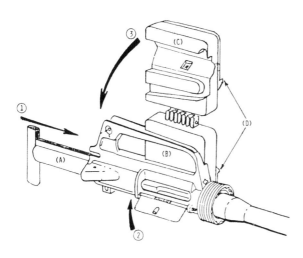

To use the AR-15/M16 Action Block, insert the upper receiver internal support (A) into upper receiver, and close the dust cover. Be sure the upper receiver internal support is all the way forward and in contact with the barrel extension. Place the upper receiver into the left half of the Action Block (B), matching the outline of the molding to the upper receiver contours. Fold the right half of the Action Block (C) down onto the right side of the upper receiver, making sure the two receiver action block halves mate properly.

standard flattop receiver halves in a vise without risk of crushing, twisting, or otherwise distorting them when applying vise pressure or torqueing the barrel nut. If you do a rebarrel with it, the Action Block has to be positioned to give sufficient clearance for the action wrench to fully engage and turn the barrel nut. The Action Block lets you tightly clamp a carry-handle receiver or flattop receiver in a large bench vise for barrel removal/installation. Torque generated while tightening the barrel nut is transmitted to the block and insert, not the receiver. The block minimizes the possibility of damage to the barrel detent pin and receiver detent notch, and it holds securely without marring the finish.

Here's the upper receiver and action block in a securely mounted bench vise. It's best to use a vise with a minimum of 3-inch or 4-inch jaws. The vise jaw ribs of the Action Block must be above, and resting on, the vise jaws. Tighten vise to secure the Block. Do Not Crush!

The Lower Receiver Vise Block is designed to lock into the magazine well on all AR-15/M16 rifles, in both normal and inverted positions.

This shows the lower receiver secured in a bench vise for all maintenance or assembly procedures.

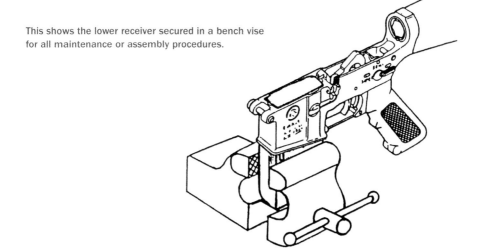

Let's start with a number: $319.99.

Yes, that is a commitment—the retail price of the **#8 120-piece Magna-Tip Professional Super Set (080-000-531WB, $320)** in early 2013. Probably as much as your wife's "CZ" engagement ring.

The Professional Super Set (PSS) is the largest selection Brownells has ever offered in a Magna-Tip set. We'll look at the PSS as the standard-setter for getting into Magna-Tip bits, then ease you into some smaller sets if you're not quite willing to choke out an "I do" for the big one.

Brownells has built the Magna-Tip driver system for quite a few years now, and the concept is pretty simple. Use a set of handles for a variety of bits rather than an individual tool for each type of screw head. It's compact, versatile, and easy to use.

The Brownells bits are specifically designed to closely fit, and therefore prevent damage to, the special types of screw heads used on firearms. Radius, parallel-ground bits, nonslip Phillips bits, extra-thin tips, extra-long shanks, square, Allen, Torx, and specialty bits are all options available to match the job and screw heads on firearms exactly.

Also, the Brownells bits are manufactured expressly for industry. They are built with the right combination of hardness and durability to give maximum strength and wear. The handles are available in a variety of lengths and styles to give you precise control, greater leverage, comfort, and speed to match your application. The bits are positively retained in the shaft by a permanent magnet or spring clip, depending on the type of handle.

Guns like this Smith & Wesson Performance Center 1911ES 45 ACP require specialty screw bits to fit decorative or specialized screw sizes, such as the grip screws in those pretty laminated panels. Every gun is different.

The Magna-Tip Professional Super-Set is the ultimate screwdriver set for professional gunsmiths, but hobbyists and tinkers can also enjoy its bounty.

A #9 22-Bit Starter Set w/ Magnetic Law Enforcement Handle (080-107-804WB, $74) eases you into the Super-Set concept with the 22 straight bits, one handle (there are others), and the heavy-duty box, and tray.

To ensure a proper fit, gunsmiths once had to grind a custom bit or screwdriver blade or wait for a specialty screwdriver to have the correct bit for a given gun screw. Proper-fitting bits prevent damage to screw slots, so when you're done, the screws are in pristine condition—a sign of professional gunsmithing.

Gun screws need a hollow-ground bit so that pressure is evenly exerted along the entire slot. An ill-fitting bit can mar the screw head and ruin the looks and value of a good firearm. Also, an improperly fitted bit or blade can gouge or scrape the gunmetal surrounding the screw.

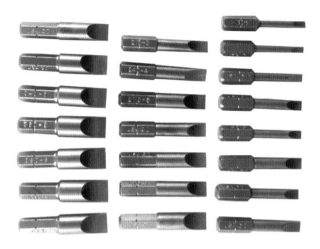

When you're ready to expand, a #10 Magna-Tip Super-Set Add-On Pak (080-108-100WB, $47) lets you upgrade it to the same configuration as the #11 44-bit Super Set.

I started with a #11 44-Bit Professional Set (080-110-801WB, $119), which covered my needs for years. I later added a Ratchet Handle and additional bits as I needed them. When I go to the range, this set goes in my toolbox. I've had people bring me their guns at the range when they saw I had the right tools for the job. I've also used this set on projects outside of the guns arena. Once you get used to not tearing up screws, you get spoiled about having the right tip for the job.

The next upgrade level is the #12 58-Bit Master Set Plus (080-112-084WB, $130). At all three levels there are Law Enforcement bit selections and your choice of clip or magnetic bit retention.

OTHER BIT COLLECTIONS

Officially Licensed NRA Magna-Tip Screwdriver Set 084-000-257WB: Bits—Hollow-Ground Steel. Handle—Shockproof plastic. 1 ¼" (3.2cm) diameter. 8" (20.3cm) OAL. Field Case—Polyethylene. Includes Slotted Bits #120-1, #150-4, #180-3, #180-5, #210-5, #240-5, #300-6 and #360-8, Leupold Windage; Hex Bits #185-00, #185-1, #185-2, #185-3, #185-4, #185-9 and #185-10; Phillips Bits #1, #2 and #3; Torx Bits T10 and TT15.

GUN-SPECIFIC MAGNA-TIP LIST

Smith & Wesson Revolvers: 120-1, 150-3, 210-2, 210-4. Colt Single Action: 180-3, 210-3, 270-3, 300-3, 340-4. Marlin 336: 180-4, 240-3, 270-3, 120-3, 300-4, 180-3. Winchester 94AE: 300-5, 445-0, 445-20, 445-10, 120-1. Ruger Black Hawk & Vaquero: 150-4, 180-3, 180-4, 210-4.Winchester '97: 180-3, 120-3, 300-3, 150-3. Winchester 92 & Rossi 92: 340-5, 210-4, 300-5, 270-4, 150-4, 180-3, 180-5. Winchester 94 Top Eject: 210-5, 180-3, 120-5, 210-3, 210-4, 300-3.

22-BIT STARTER SUPER-SET

#120-3, #120-5, #150-4, #150-6, #180-3, #180-5, #210-4, #210-6, #240-3, #240-5, #240-7, #270-4, #270-6, #300-3, #300-5, #300-7, #340-4, #340-6, #340-8,#360-3, #360-5, #360-7.

44-BIT SUPER-SET PLUS

#120-3, #120-4, #120-5, #120-6, #150-3, #150-4, #150-5, #150-6, #180-3, #180-4, #180-5, #180-6, #210-3, #210-4, #210-5, #210-6, #210-7, #240-3, #240-4, #240-5, #240-6, #240-7, #270-3, #270-4, #270-5, #270-6, #270-7, #300-3, #300-4, #300-5, #300-6, #300-7, #340-3, #340-4, #340-5, #340-6, #340-7, #340-8, #360-3, #360-4, #360-5, #360-6, #360-7, #360-8.

58-BIT MASTER SUPER-SET PLUS

Adds 10 hex-head bits (#185-9, #185-10, #185-00, #185-0, #185-1, #185-2, #185-3, #185-4, #185-5, #185-6), 3 Phillips-head bits (#440-1, #440-2, #440-0), and a ⅛" square bit for Remington butt plates to the contents of the 44 Bit Super Set Plus.

Made from hardened steel, these bits are hollow-ground for a no-slip seat in the screw slot. Hollow ground means metal is relieved above the tip, so the blade fits into the slot to its full depth.

The set includes 75 straight, 4 Phillips, 17 hex (Allen), 11 Torx, and 13 specialty bits for sights, scope mounts, grip bushings, Ruger ejectors, and other unique applications, plus the handy Magna-Tip Choke Tube Wrench and a hex-to-square adapter that lets you use your Magna-Tip handles to drive ¼ inch drive sockets.

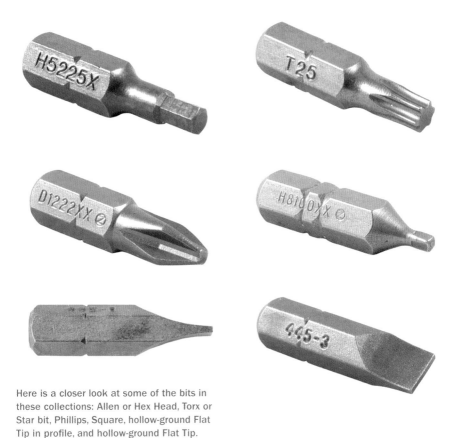

Here is a closer look at some of the bits in these collections: Allen or Hex Head, Torx or Star bit, Phillips, Square, hollow-ground Flat Tip in profile, and hollow-ground Flat Tip.

The Magna-Tip Professional Super Set comes with seven different handles of various lengths and configurations. Two of the handles have a hollow section to allow the user to throw in a few bits to conveniently take to the range. Besides the six fixed handles, there is a dandy ratcheting handle with a T-shaped grip that is ideal for use on scope rings and such. The Magna-Tip produces a lock-and-load-style snap when bit meets shank. The shank seems to suck the bit in after only about 4mm of insertion.

Several specialty bits fit screws like S&W rear sight nuts and Ruger scope ring-to-base clamp screws. Also included is a square-tip bit and a special bit to remove and install grip screw bushings on 1911-style pistols.

The kit's seven driver handles ensure you have the handle best suited to any situation. You get the full-size #81 Handle, #84 Hollow Handle, magnetic Law Enforcement Handle, Law Enforcement Hollow Handle, Compact Law Enforcement Handle, the popular Stubby, and the Magna-Tip Ratchet Handle.

All of the bits and handles reside in a synthetic Delrin bench block that allows handy access.

The Professional Super Set is the most versatile screwdriver system you'll ever use—and quite possibly the last one you'll ever have to buy.

Car mechanics will recognize the underlying design of the **#13 Magna-Tip Ratchet Handle (080-000-513, $35)** Just marry a Snap-On brand T-handle screwdriver with a ratcheting function.

Use is simple: plug in the appropriate Magna-Tip bit, and the handle's heavy-duty ratcheting mechanism provides three-way operation to tighten or loosen in clockwise and counter-clockwise directions, respectively, and in a locked mode where you don't need to ratchet.

For most gun jobs, I prefer this Ratchet Handle to the standard high-impact-plastic Magna-Tip handle. Because of tennis elbow (aka computer workplace elbow), it's painful for me to grasp a handle and turn it repeatedly. The ratcheting driver provides extra leverage like on a conventional T-handle driver, so I can quickly tighten or loosen almost any gun screw.

Caution: When using this tool with slotted or Phillips-head fasteners, ensure you choose the correct bit and make sure it remains centered in the slot at all times. This will help prevent the bit slipping out of and chewing the slot edges or marring surrounding surfaces.

The rounded T-shaped handgrip is contoured to ensure maximum comfort and control. And it's faster—the stainless-steel shank keeps the bits precisely centered, and a powerful magnet retains the bits. That means you don't need to lift the tool from the work to reposition it for each turn, as with standard screwdrivers.

The ratchet handle has a high-impact plastic handle and stainless steel shank. It's 5 ½ inches long overall, with a 3 ⅝-inch-long shank. The handle is 3 inches wide at its widest point, providing exceptional leverage and speed. It accepts ¼-inch hex bits, including all Magna-Tip bits.

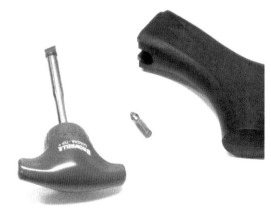

Besides using the handle on guns, my son uses the ratcheting handle when he's upgrading or working on our Apple desktop or laptop computers. Those machines have very small Torx and socket head fasteners on the logic boards and drive bays, so when he's putting machines back together, he will turn the shank with his fingers to start the ratcheting action and keep the fastener from reversing with the motion of the handle. After enough threads are engaged, he turns the ratchet handle and zippety-zips things together. The only thing faster is an electric driver.

Tip: If you're working against a fastener that's anchored to something in a vise, grasp the handle in the Locked position through the middle and ring fingers. Then press your fingers into your belt or belly and twist your torso one direction or the other. This supplies a few degrees of super leverage rather than turning the handle just with your forearm muscles.

Adjustable in 1-inch/pound increments, the **#14 Magna-Tip Adjustable Torque Handle (080-000-515, $150)** lets me apply the exact amount of torque necessary for any gun screw, from scope rings to trigger guard screws.

I use a torque handle to reset the action screws in my deer rifle when I have to take the barreled action off the stock.

It's adjustable from 10 to 70 in-lbs. in 1 in-lb. increments to eliminate guesswork and prevent under- or over-tightening screws. The ⅜ inch square drive bit locks positively to the included socket adapter to let you use any Magna-Tip bit. The adapter's clip-style chuck grasps the bit securely to prevent slipping or falling out.

The streamlined, teardrop-shaped torque handle, left, provides a secure grip for maximum leverage and even transfer of tightening force. To change torque setting, lift the handle, turn it to the desired setting indicated through the window scale, and push back in until it snaps firmly into place.

A self-limiting clutch "clicks" free when the specified amount of torque is reached, preventing further tightening and possible damage to components. The rubber-coated aluminum body provides additional gripping surface and protects against scratches. To protect the precision tool from bumps and help maintain its accuracy, a hard-sided case is included.

The streamlined, teardrop-shaped torque handle, left, provides a secure grip for maximum leverage and even transfer of tightening force. To change torque setting, lift the handle, turn it to the desired setting indicated through the window scale, and push back in until it snaps firmly into place.

If you've ever had your AR-15 go "click" when it was supposed to go "bang," then you'll want to take a close look at the items in this **#15 AR-15 Field Parts Kit (078-060-015WB, $71)**.

The convenient, pre-packaged kit contains selected DPMS and Yellow Tavern Custom Shoppe parts most often required for emergency field repairs. Chances are you'll have what you need to keep a malfunction from spoiling your hunt or ruining a match.

Many gun owners question how to handle the different kinds of pins in their guns. They often want to know if their punches are the right ones, or if they can use a slightly different one without damaging their pins. Usually, the answer is no.

One of the easiest ways to mar an otherwise nice finish is to use the wrong punch to remove a certain pin. Even a light tap on a hammer can send the wrong punch skittering over a deeply blued finish, and it's all so unnecessary. Punches are inexpensive compared to many other tools, and for their utility, they're lightweight and compact, so having the right punch for your guns' pins is fairly easy.

Some of the included items in the Field Parts Kit are a pivot pin and spring; bolt gas rings, pins, and catch spring; a buffer retainer spring and CAR and STD buffer springs; an ejector, ejector pins and spring, and an ejection port cover spring; an extractor and extractor spring and pin; and a firing pin and firing-pin retaining pins.

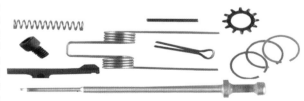

Also, the punches can be used for other jobs, such as removing/installing the rear sight on a Glock if you don't want to buy a specialized tool for that task. The nylon tip won't leave any marks on the sight base.

The **#16 6-Way Nylon/Brass Punch Set (080-475-106WB, $24)** is a collection of indispensable, non-marring punches. Common to all the kits are high-impact steel handles with knurled grips, which make holding and controlling interchangeable tips easy and consistent. The handles are built to withstand heavy impact with a minimum of distortion.

Two types of interchangeable and replaceable tips fit the handles. Nylon tips have steel reinforcing pins that prevent bending or breaking. They provide completely mar-free punching action. Brass tips are harder than nylon but softer than steel. They can be used where slight discoloration is acceptable.

What's particularly great about this set is its life span. Brass and nylon punches for sights and large pins do bend, break, and deform. You can dress the tips, but eventually they will have to be replaced. With this set you get a sturdy, easy-to-hold handle, so

These punches will handle many pin types. The threaded brass and nylon tips screw into the handle, offering a bigger gripping or driving surface than most standard punches. If you think a punch set isn't needed, here are just the pins for a 1911 auto rebuild: hammer strut pin, link pin, mainspring plunger, sear pin, ejector pin, mainspring housing pin, mainspring plunger, mainspring plunger retainer, hammer pin, slide stop plunger, and thumb safety plunger.

when the tips can no longer be dressed, just buy a new tip. As a plus, it is possible to shape a brass or aluminum tip to suit a specific use, like matching the side of a sight.

Filing is serious business. When you're removing wood or metal or some other material, we ain't in Kansas anymore, Toto.

But the need to file off, file down, and file out items is surprisingly large and varied. Interior parts on new guns may need just a touch of dressing to work properly. A burr may arise. The sharp edge on a rail may need to be broken. And on and on.

The **#17 File Starter Set (080-803-000, $400)** is a complete set for the novice gunsmith. Also included are accessories that enable the gun owner to use and maintain the new files safely and with maximum efficiency.

There are too many jobs and too many uses for these files to cover everything here. But we can cover some general advice about using these files and how to care for them.

The larger file handles included in the set are adjustable and should be used on the larger files in the set. The small black handles fit the needle files. Thoroughly clean new files with a solvent, such as TCE cleaner degreaser, to remove any traces of preservative oil applied by the manufacturer. If oil or grease is left on the file it will cause metal chips removed during filing to stick or lodge between the file teeth (this is known as "pinning"). Pinning inhibits the cutting effectiveness of the file and will score or scratch the surface of the work piece.

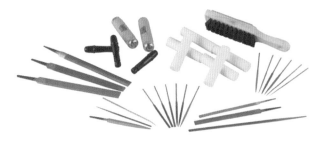

Items contained in File Starter Kit: Needle File Set (fine), 3 Square Bent 60° File, 60° Sight Base File, 4-inch Barrette File (#1 cut), 8-inch Half-Round File (smooth cut), 8-inch Mill File (smooth cut), 8-inch Hand File (smooth cut), 6-inch Pillar File (#2 cut), 8-inch Extra Narrow Pillar File (#2 cut), 4-inch Very Extra Narrow Pillar File (#2 cut), 6 Pack File Chalk, Double Face File Card, 3 Needle File Handles, 2 Adjustable File Handles. Always use an appropriate file handle whenever you use any size or shape file. File handles help you hold the file more securely and protect your hand from accidental injury caused by sharp, exposed file tangs. File handles lessen hand and arm fatigue and give you more control of the file for more consistent, even cutting strokes, which will improve the look, accuracy, and final result of your work.

Rub file chalk into the file teeth after degreasing the file. The chalk collects between the teeth and helps prevent metal chips from sticking and building up on the file. To apply file chalk, simply rake the chalk back and forth along the face of the file. One or two strokes will apply sufficient chalk.

To learn to file correctly takes a small amount of application and practice. When using your files, never pull the file backward across the work piece. Push forward to cut, and then lift the file clear of the work piece on the return stroke. These files will cut on the forward stroke only. Pulling the files backward across the work piece will roll the sharp edges of the file teeth and quickly dull the file. Filing hardened or plated metal will also quickly dull your files.

A file card is a double-sided brush with fine nylon bristles on one side and bent steel bristles on the other. It is specially made to clean filing residue from between the file teeth. Use the file card frequently to keep the file teeth clean and clear of chips as you are working. Keeping the file teeth clean will enhance the cutting efficiency and smoothness of the cut. Thoroughly clean your files with the file card after every use and before putting them away. Rechalk the file after each cleaning.

Files should be stored so the faces of the files never contact or touch one another. Contact between the files can lead to chipped, broken or damaged teeth. You may wish to make up individual "sheaths" of cardboard or plastic for your files if they are to be stored in a toolbox.

Included in the File Kit is the Brownells File Storage Block, which will hold and separate the individual files and prevent damage to the teeth.

As with the #1 Basic Gunsmith Kit, this may be too much for your needs. To build a file collection over time, you can start with the Economy Needle File Set (345-475-000WB, $27), the Professional Gunsmith Needle File Medium Set (249-210-010WB, $121), or the Professional Gunsmith Needle File Fine Set (249-210-030WB, $110). Or you can buy individual file types as you need them.

The seven-function **#18 AR-15 Multi-Tool by DPMS (231-000-007, $34)** lets you build and repair AR-15s without cluttering your shop table or range bag. The brawny DPMS powder-coated steel wrench combines seven tools in one for maintenance, building, or repair of AR-15 series rifles. It's well thought out from one end to the other.

The seven functions of the #18 AR-15 Multi-Tool by DPMS cover major maintenance operations for the AR-15.

A semi-circular cutout with an inset area fits collapsible stocks.

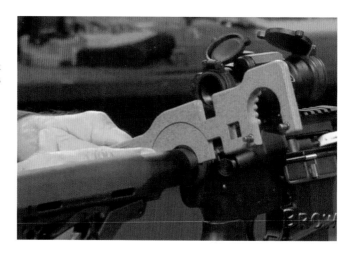

A ¾-inch square slot on the top of the wrench makes changing out compensators simple.

A wide hole in one end of the wrench keeps it handy. Hang it flat on a wall peg in your work area, and you'll always know where it is. A big-slot screwdriver head makes removing buttstock screws a snap. A semi-circular cutout with an inset area fits collapsible stocks. A ¾-inch-square slot on the top of the wrench makes changing out compensators simple. Opposite the compensator slot is a ⅝-inch wrench slot that fits buttstock tubes. Next is a half-inch-square hole for a socket or torque wrench. A ridged slot will remove and install peg-style barrel nuts and standard barrel nuts. Pins on the front of the Multi-Tool will help install and disassemble free float tubes.

Serious shooters who are on the go want a simple but versatile set of tools to perform general field repair and maintenance on a variety of firearm types. The **#19 Basic Field Tool Kit by Brownells (080-000-665, $213)** is what they're looking for.

This Basic Field Tool Kit contains a specially configured Magna-Tip screwdriver set with #81 handle, polyethylene case, and bench tray filled with 23 of the most commonly used slotted, hex, Phillips, and Torx bits. This selection will handle the majority of gun screws in existence.

An additional miniature screwdriver set gives you six double-ended Phillips, slotted, and Torx quick-change bits to take care of small but critical gun fasteners. And the knurled swivel-top driver handle provides fingertip control to prevent gouging or losing those really tiny screws.

These common steel, starter, and pin punches will easily start, remove, and install spring pins and roll pins in most guns without damage to the pin or firearm itself. The steel punches are individually marked for size. Also included is a non-marring, nylon drift punch.

There's almost five pounds of tools packed in the black or coyote brown 1000-denier Cordura field cases. Individual tool pouches inside the cases keep everything protected and organized.

An extra-long, buttstock screwdriver makes removing most shotgun stocks fast and easy.

A smooth-cut file with handle allows you to perform minor metal-removal jobs. Four additional handle inserts accept many other file sizes you may wish to add.

A medium-grit India stone allows you to lap, hone, sharpen, or polish out small metal imperfections.

Additional tools include: a steel packing hook for releasing springs; a pair of 6-inch chain-nose pliers for grabbing and holding small parts; a nylon bench block with "V" center; a nylon/brass hammer; and a double-ended gun parts cleaning brush. And to safeguard your gun's finish during cleaning or repair, there's a soft, flexible neoprene gun mat included.

Felo (pronounced "fellow") is one of the leading specialists for quality screwdrivers and bits in Germany, and its **#20 Precision Screwdriver Kit (123-000-018WB, $35)** demonstrates why. This kit employs a handle driver system that accepts six interchangeable steel shafts with twelve precision-ground bits for fast change from standard slot blade to Phillips or Torx tip. It works great on many small parts and accessories found on most guns and optics.

A collet lets you adjust the shaft length approximately 3" to get to those hard-to-reach places. The rotating cap minimizes friction to ease screw removal or installation, while the hanging hole in the handle can be used with a second shaft as a T-handle for extra leverage to remove stubborn screws.

Reversible precision blades make up the rest of the kit, with $\frac{5}{64}$- to $\frac{9}{64}$-inch slotted sizes, PH0-PH1 and PH000-PH00 Phillips blades, and T6-T15,

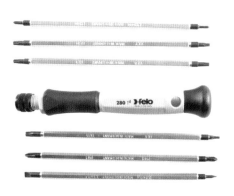

The Felo screwdrivers have handles that allow three-finger precision use, helped by a freely rotating cap. A pleasant soft-grip outer material adds comfort.

T7-T10, and T8-T9 Torx blades. They're manufactured from chromemolyb-denumvanadium steel and have hardened black tips for precision fit.

The **#21 Surge Multi-Tool by Leatherman Tool Group (525-000-002WB, $90)** is one of the company's two largest multi-tools. The Surge was built for tough jobs, perfect for your grab-and-go bag, range bag, briefcase, or vehicle glove compartment. The 21-in-1 general-purpose tool will also carry on your belt or as MOLLE gear with the included nylon sheath.

The 12.5-ounce Surge is a powerhouse, built with Leatherman Tools' largest pliers, longest multi-tool blades, and easy-to-use locks. It measures 4 ½ inches long when folded and 6 inches overall when extended.

The Surge deploys needle nose and regular pliers along with wire cutters, hard-wire cutters, stranded-wire cutters, an electrical crimper, and a wire stripper. Cutting implements include a knife and serrated knife, a saw, and scissors.

There are two files, one for wood and metal and a diamond-coated choice for hardened surfaces. There's a large screwdriver, along with large-

Throughout the Multi-Tool, hardened steel pivots ensure smooth, reliable operation, and thumbnail tabs easily swing the tools out of the handle. Surge tools include needle nose and regular pliers, wire cutters, hard-wire cutters, stranded-wire cutters, an electrical crimper, and a wire stripper. Cutting implements include a knife and serrated knife, a saw, and scissors.

and small-bit drivers. Rounding out the tools are a unique blade exchanger, an awl with thread loop, a 9-inch ruler, a bottle opener, and a can opener.

Rich Langner invented the first practical laser boresighter more than ten years ago. Today, his company manufactures thousands of Sitelite Laser Boresighters every year, because the laser systems save hunters and shooters a lot of headaches, ammo, and time at the range.

The **#22 SL-500 Ultra-Mag Laser Boresighter by Site-Lite (100-004-085WB, $250)** allows you to zero your scope to point-of-aim at 100 yards before you ever head for the range. There are three models, but I prefer the SL-500, which uses an ultra-bright green laser that is 50 to 100 times brighter than red lasers, and is much easier to see in daylight. An included CR123 lithium battery powers it.

The Laser Boresighters use super-strength rare-earth magnets to hold the laser securely within the rifle bore for consistent accuracy. They fit .22- to .50-caliber bores plus 20- and 12-gauge shotguns without extra arbors or sleeves.

An anodized aircraft-quality aluminum housing contains the laser, which is precisely aligned to the center of the bore. Various O-rings guide the precision stainless-steel muzzle adapter into the bore, and no metal ever touches the barrel's rifling.

A calibrated target is used at 25 feet to sight-in for 100 yards. Quick and easy to use, just place the special laser target 25 feet away and aim the laser at

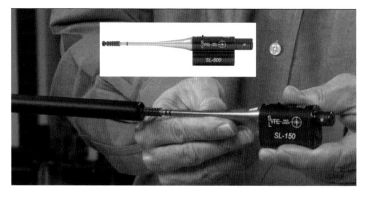

This is the Ultra-Mag SL-150 unit (inset) being inserted, and both it and the regular SL-100 are fine choices for most jobs. I prefer the green light of the SL-500 that can be seen at any time of day easily 100+ yards away. The SL-500 is a huge time and money saver if I'm at the range with several firearms and trying to zero multiple ammo/rifle/calibers. On most rifles, handguns, and slug shotguns, I'm often dead on, or may need only a single shot to verify zero.

it, then adjust the scope till the crosshairs align with the target. The bore-sighters work equally well with red-dot scopes and iron sights.

Use the SL-100 Standard Model indoors, where you have control over ambient lighting. It's powered by two #357/LR-44 batteries, which are included. The SL-150 Ultra-Mag has a super-bright 635mm laser for better visibility in bright, ambient light conditions. It's powered by one CR2 lithium battery, which is included.

The **#23 Electronic Trigger Pull Gauge by Lyman (539-000-005, $68)** is the perfect tool for target shooters, silhouette shooters, gunsmiths, hunters, or anyone else who wants to adjust their trigger-pull weights accurately and easily. There are no weights or sliding pointers to worry about. Just place the hook on the trigger and pull.

The Lyman gauge is easy to use and takes the guesswork out of adjusting or comparing triggers. I prefer to use the gauge when the gun is secured in the #5 Battenfeld Best Gun Vise 100-012-229WB or wedged between

If you tinker with triggers, the #23 Electronic Trigger Pull Gauge by Lyman 539-000-005 is a must. If you plan on doing anything to a trigger, you have to know where you started and where you end up as far as trigger weight. The Lyman is accurate and repeatable. If you think you can guess weights or feel changes in weight, guess again. The 9-volt battery lasts a long time—I've used mine for five years and haven't changed the battery yet. The ballistic-nylon carrying case protects it inside my range box.

sandbags at the range. I believe the gauge works better when the "L" of the rod faces away from the LCD display.

The Digital Trigger Pull Gauge is equipped with a large, easy-to-read LCD display and is pushbutton operated for zero, clear, and averaging functions, giving results in digital pounds or kilograms. You can also take multiple readings, and the Digital Trigger Pull Gauge will tell you the average weight for the string.

State-of-the-art strain-gauge technology allows for 0.1-ounce accuracy from 1 ounce to 5 pounds and half-ounce accuracy from 5 to 12 pounds.

CHAPTER 2

CLEANERS AND MAINTENANCE GADGETS

In shooting, as in hygiene, cleanliness is next to godliness. Of the gadgets most important to the long-term happy function of your firearms, keeping them cleaned and lubricated is probably the most important maintenance job for the shooter. And there are some other related maintenance supplies that assist you once your firearms are cleaned and lubed properly. To get started, we'll look at systems or kits first, since they have all the components for ongoing maintenance you'll need.

The **#24 All-In-One Gun Cleaning System by Brownells (080-000-588WB, $384)** contains everything you need to thoroughly clean rifles, handguns, and shotguns to ensure peak reliability and accuracy. These comprehensive kits are filled with the best cleaning components, and they're packed in a rugged polymer storage/carry box with a roomy top compartment and four pullout drawers.

Inside you'll find top-quality nylon-coated Dewey cleaning rods that won't scratch bores or damage rifling. The All-In-One System includes 11-inch and 36-inch cleaning rods for .17- to .22-caliber firearms, a 12-inch centerfire pistol rod, a 36-inch centerfire rifle rod, a 34-inch one-piece shotgun rod, and a nylon cleaning rod storage sleeve. (I would add appropriate bore guides for the rods.)

Swab the bore with Shooter's Choice bore cleaner and attach Brownells Special Line bore brushes with pure phosphor bronze wire bristles to loosen copper, lead, and powder fouling. Then use the included mops and all-cotton flannel patches to provide a vigorous yet gentle cleaning.

Add #31 Brownells Advantage CLP to the supplied bronze chamber brushes to help you remove carbon fouling that leads to extraction problems. For problem areas, the kit contains some Brownells TCE Cleaner/Degreaser.

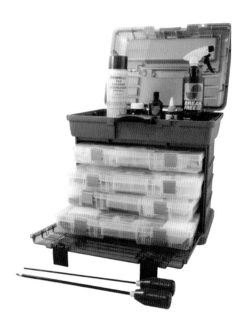

This is a hoss of a system, and may be overkill for most shooters. The upside is that it will take care of nearly any firearm-cleaning chore, but if you need to add other specialty items, such as an AR chamber brush, the system will accommodate them in one place.

It cuts through grease, wax, and gunk, even silicones, lifts them away, and dries clean with little to no residue.

To keep the workspace clean, included are a 12-inch-by-24-inch bench mat and six shop cloths.

Remington's Fast Snap Rifle, Shotgun, and Pistol Cleaning Kits contain everything you need to keep your firearms in pristine condition, and their compact sizes allow you to carry them in a range bag or backpack. Each kit includes plastic-coated cleaning cables with a comfortable, easy-to-grasp

The compact arrangement of the cleaning supplies makes this kit portable. The bore lights are what set these kits apart from most other cleaning kits. They make examining the chamber and muzzle areas much easier.

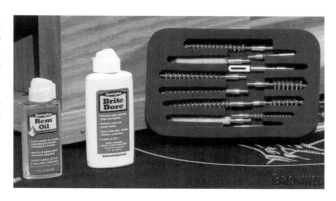

Fast Snap T-handle, a 1-ounce bottle of Rem Oil, a 2-ounce bottle of Brite Bore fouling solvent, and an assortment of bronze brushes, bore mops, patch loops, and patches.

An easy-to-use polymer bore light with interchangeable straight and 90-degree necks projects a bright light for easy inspection of bores, chambers, and other hard-to-see areas. The quarter-inch-diameter lens illuminates bores from .22 caliber to .45 caliber, and the light runs on a handy AAA battery.

All of the components fit in a reinforced hard-sided canvas case with a foam interior. The case is about 7 inches long and 3 inches thick, and it's 4 ½ inches wide. Separate slots for each piece keeps everything organized.

The **#25 Remington Fast Snap Rifle Cleaning Kit (768-000-021WB, $36)** includes two non-scratching cleaning cables. The one for .22-caliber bores and up is 32 inches long. The one for .17-caliber air rifles and cartridge rifles measures 26 inches in length. Other items in this kit include three brass patch loops and bronze bore brushes in .17, .22, .25, .270, .30, .375,

Remington Fast Snap Rifle Cleaning Kit.

Remington Fast Snap Shotgun Cleaning Kit.

Remington Fast Snap Pistol Cleaning Kit.

and .45 calibers. There are also .22- and .30-caliber bore mops, and 75 square cleaning patches in 1 ⅛-inch, 1 ½-inch, and 2-inch sizes.

The **#25a Remington Fast Snap Shotgun Cleaning Kit (768-000-020, $40)** has a longer 39-inch cleaning cable. There are also two brass patch loops and .410-bore, 20-gauge, and 12-gauge bronze bore brushes and cotton bore mops. A set of 75 2-inch-square cleaning patches rounds out the components.

The **#25b Remington Fast Snap Pistol Cleaning Kit (768-000-022, $40)** includes a revolver-cylinder cleaning adapter along with two cleaning cables, one 12 inches long and the other 24 inches long. There are two brass patch loops, and bronze bore brushes and cotton bore mops in .22, .357/9mm, .40, and .45 calibers. Rounding out the kit are 75 square cleaning patches in 1 ⅛-inch, 1 ½-inch, and 2-inch sizes.

The kits above are great, full-service products that will serve most shooters well. However, for many guns I own, I continue to downscale my cleaning kits to the bare essentials, which means a general bore cleaner, lubri-

Brownells carries many sizes of Bore Snakes, from 17 to 50 caliber, plus shotgun-gauge diameters. One pass through most barrels will do the trick. I have found it best to make a Zip-Loc bag in each caliber I own, which carries a properly sized Bore Snake and small containers of spray solvent and lubricating oil. The Zip-Loc has the Snake's diameter written on it for easy reference. If you don't want to make your own, Hoppe's makes a similar package that includes a Bore Snake, Hoppe's No. 9 Solvent, Hoppe's Lubricating Oil, Hoppe's Weatherguard Cloths, and a pulling tool.

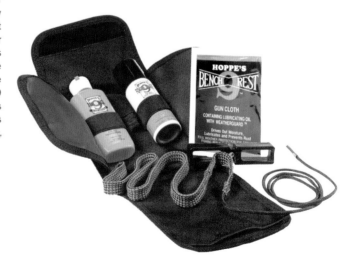

cant, and a pull-through cleaning system such as the **#26 Hoppe's Bore Snakes (664-100-257WB, $20)**.

The Bore Snakes allow the shooter to do thorough single-step cleanups of dirty firearms, and I started using this product first on my .25-06 Rem. deer rifle, which has a tight Lothar Walther barrel on it. When I was working up loads for it, I'd shoot ten then clean—a process made very easy by removing the bolt, sticking the extension nozzle on a can of #31 Brownells Advantage CLP into the chamber, spraying a blast, then dropping the Snake weight from chamber to muzzle, and pulling through. Ten shots later, rinse and repeat.

The heavy-duty pull-through cleaning system is made of braided nylon with built-in phosphor-bronze bristle brushes. SOP for using a Snake has the shooter apply bore cleaner to the front of the Snake, and oil to the end of the cord, and drop the weighted-brass end down the bore. Then he pulls the Snake through, cleaning and lubricating the barrel bore in a single step.

On most guns, I usually run a Snake through once and the barrel is squeaky clean. Twice if needed. The expanded surface area on the Snake is like running thirty patches through, so it cuts cleaning time dramatically. I have read that some users say the Snakes can break if the bore fit is too tight, but I've horsed them through rifles, pistols, and shotguns and haven't broken one yet. When I can't budge one, I pull on the back end (loop end) of the snake (or even step on it) so that it stretches out and passes through.

One thing I like about Hoppe's Bore Snakes is the metal tip on the ends of the pull-through cords. This keeps the cord from fraying after many uses and works as a weight to drop the cord through the barrel. If you are cleaning the bore using the proper procedure and inserting the end of the snake from the chamber end to come out the muzzle, you'll understand how valuable this weight feature is.

Otis makes a pair of specialty cleaning kits which I've come to like: the **#27 Sniper Rifle Cleaning Kit for 308/7.62mm Sniper Rifles (668-000-027, $107)**, and the **#28 AR-15 Grip Cleaning Kit (668-000-005, $64)**.

The Otis Cleaning Kit for 308/7.62mm Sniper Rifles is a portable military-issue system that contains all the components needed to thoroughly

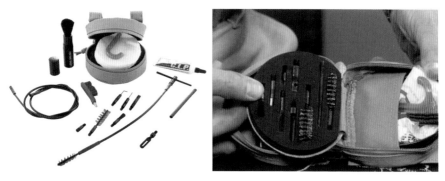

The kit's 8 ounces of gear replaces more than 3 pounds of conventional cleaning supplies. It all fits into a zippered MOLLE-compatible case with a tight-weave, waterproof Dark Earth nylon shell. The case can be clipped to a belt.

clean the DMR-M14. It's also sized for many other .30-caliber rifles, including the M24, M40, M240, M1, and AK-47.

Inside, a flexible 30 inch long cleaning cable allows thorough breech-to-muzzle cleaning. A separate, more manageable 8-inch cable can be used to clean the receiver. Both coil up neatly for storage in the case. All brass fittings on the cables and the other brass components have a matte-black finish so you don't unwittingly expose your location.

Elsewhere in the kit, you'll find a .30-caliber bronze-bristle bore brush and chamber brush, a slotted tip for patches, and a half-ounce tube of Mil-Spec CLP that cleans, lubes, and protects against corrosion.

Use the included scraper and the straight and angled locking-lug picks for cleaning bolt faces and locking lug recesses. Plus there's a retractable lens brush for optics, an all-purpose nylon utility brush, and complete instructions.

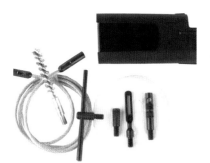

The Grip Kit Cleaning System for AR-style 5.56mm rifles is only 1 ¼ inches wide, just over 3 inches tall, and a half-inch thick, making it the most compact cleaning kit available for your AR-15, M4, or M16 rifle.

Rounding out the components are ten cleaning patches, a T-handle bar and base, a NATO thread adapter, a nylon end brush, and a combo fiber-optic bore reflector and safety flag.

Many AR-15s have collapsible CAR-style buttstocks without trap doors in the butt plates, so you can't store cleaning kits there. The Otis Grip Kit fits into a plastic sleeve, which then locks into place in Mil-Spec hollow handgrips. It comes with a 26-inch Memory Flex Cable, obstruction removers, slotted tips, T-handle, 5.56 NATO bronze bore brush, and cleaning patches.

In the **#29 Brownells AR-15/M16 Professional Cleaning System (080-000-573WB, $150)**, Brownells brings you premium-quality components for detailed cleaning of your entire 5.56 NATO/223 Remington MSR.

For the bore, there's a top-quality 36-inch Dewey cleaning rod long enough for any AR-15 barrel, twelve Special Line bronze bore brushes, and deep-scrubbing all-cotton, flannel patches, plus tools specifically developed for the AR-15. The rod comes with a jag and an 8-32 thread adapter.

A hold-open link separates the upper and lower receivers and locks them in place so you can clean the bore and chamber the correct way, from the breech. A rugged Delrin plastic bore guide centers the cleaning rod in the bore and protects the rifling from damage, and silicone O-rings in the bore guide seal the chamber and keep solvent out of the action and trigger.

For the upper receiver, there's a combo cleaning tool that has a properly sized bronze brush and cotton mop to let you scrub away stubborn carbon fouling from the bolt carrier way and lug recesses. Then there's the combina-

This convenient, professional-grade cleaning system contains everything you need to ensure your AR operates with peak reliability and accuracy, allowing you to detail all parts of your rifle's operating system, including bore, chamber, gas system, and bolt carrier way.

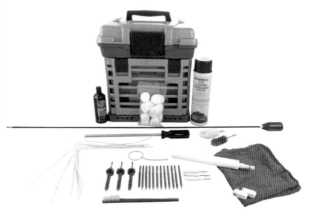

tion bronze-and-stainless-steel chamber brush, originally designed for the M16, which digs out fouling that can hinder extraction.

All the gear in the #29 Brownells AR-15/M16 Professional Cleaning System comes packed in a rugged plastic storage/carry box. In the box are a roomy top compartment and three slide-out drawers with plenty of storage space for extra items. Other items in the kit include cotton bore mops, gas tube cleaners, shop cloths, a 4-ounce can of Break Free CLP Cleaner, and a 24-ounce can of TCE Cleaner/Degreaser.

The **#30 AR-15/M16 Deluxe Buttstock Cleaning Kit (084-000-233WB, $22)** is a more portable unit designed by the Military/Law Enforcement Group at Brownells. Packaged in a heavy Nylon pouch designed to conform perfectly to the taper of the storage compartment of A-1 and A-2 style buttstocks, the AR-15/M16 Buttstock Cleaning Kit fits snugly to ensure the gun stays rattle-free. There's a government-type five-piece cleaning rod,

Though the #30 AR-15/M16 Deluxe Buttstock Cleaning Kit is portable, all this will still fit inside A1- and A2- style buttstocks without rattling.

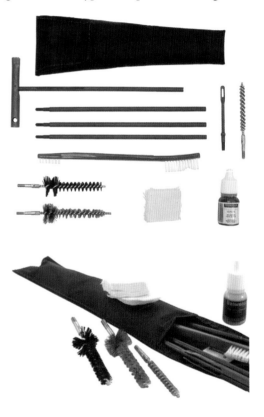

CLP's specially formulated synthetic oils won't lose viscosity, dry out, or stiffen in extreme environments such as cold, heat, dust, dirt, humidity, and salt air.

bronze bore and chamber brushes, and a double-ended parts cleaning brush packaged with detailed instructions to guide shooters through the cleaning process. It also includes a solvent-resistant Nylon chamber brush, 25-Pak of Mil-Spec cleaning patches, and ¼ oz. of Brownells Friction Defense Gun Oil.

In addition to the packages above, there are some specialized supplies I think are worth having in your gunroom. First among them is **#31 Brownells Advantage CLP (080-000-817WB, $13).**

Brownells' Advantage CLP is an acronym for a unique formulation of synthetic oils and individual proprietary ingredients that clean, lubricate, and protect metal. CLP is recognized around the world as the standard by which maximum metal performance and protection is ensured.

CLP penetrates and spreads along metal surfaces into every pit and crevice to undercut contamination and lift residue away where it can be removed. It leaves a long-lasting lubricating film that dramatically reduces adhesion of sand, grit, or other abrasives, which cause wear and failure. Also, corrosion inhibitors prevent the formation of rust while CLP's unique boundary film protects metal surfaces from moisture and other contaminants.

Wipe-Out contains corrosion inhibitors so you can leave the cleaner in the bore for up to 24 hours. It won't harm modern gunstock finishes, carbon steel, or stainless steel, and it contains no acid or ammonia. The snout helps keep the foam contained when you apply it directly to an orifice or when you use the extender.

Another cleaner I like is **#32 Sharp Shoot R Wipe-Out (100-001-388WB, $9)** brushless bore-cleaning foam, which dissolves carbon, copper, brass, bronze, black powder, and smokeless powder fouling.

I have used most of the various chemical cleaners in the past, starting many years ago with Hoppe's #9 to Sweet's and all of the latest from Butch's.

After cleaning my rifles as thoroughly as I previously thought possible with Copper Cleaners and Butch's Bore Shine, I decided to give Wipe-Out a try. After the first soaking, I found significant copper fouling.

The 5-ounce aerosol can puts out powerful foam that suspends and then absorbs fouling for superb cleaning. It also removes antique finishes such as varnish, shellac, oil, and lacquer.

The heavy metals, chemicals, and solvents casual shooters and professionals come into contact with need specialized, thorough cleaning. To decontaminate surfaces and skin, Brownells sells two Hygenall-brand cleaning products that are approved and licensed by the Centers for Disease Control and Prevention: **#33 ToxOff**

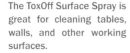

More effective than soap and water, the FieldWipes also remove dirt and grime while killing germs.

The ToxOff Surface Spray is great for cleaning tables, walls, and other working surfaces.

Surface Decon & All Purpose Cleaner Spray (100-006-993WB, $15); and #34 FieldWipes (100-006-928WB, $15).

The ToxOff Surface Spray removes toxic heavy metals from surfaces. Spray it on to decontaminate surfaces after exposure to heavy metals such as lead, hexavalent, chromium, mercury, cadmium, and other cationic metals.

Hygenall FieldWipes help prevent transfer of lead and toxic chemicals to other surfaces and people, especially children. Each canister contains 45 disposable FieldWipes, which leave skin feeling clean and refreshed. The FieldWipes are made of non-toxic ingredients and do not contain benzalkonium chloride, EDTA, or betaines.

The FieldWipes are convenient to use after shooting firearms or handling ammunition, and they remove more than 99 percent of unseen lead particles as well as toxic dust from arsenic, cadmium, mercury, zinc, hex chrome, depleted uranium oxide, tungsten, and other heavy metals.

#35 J-B Bore Cleaner by Brownells (083-065-002, $10) is the original formula developed by Jim Brobst and produced under exclusive license to Brownells. J-B has been a favorite of gunsmiths for years, because the pros know that a good scrubbing with J-B often restores accuracy. After shooting season is over I run this through my bore. It gets everything out. I shoot moly-coated bullets, and it even gets all the moly out.

After doing its work (see next page for detailed instructions), J-B easily wipes out of the bore, leaving behind no abrasive residue which might keep "cutting" after you've finished cleaning. Though J-B Bore Cleaner is widely used by match and varmint rifle shooters who put a lot of rounds down range, you can also use J-B with Lewis Lead Remover to get the last speck of leading out of pistol bores. J-B also cleans out lead, powder, and plastic foul-

Bench rest shooting champion and Trinidad State Junior College Gunsmithing Instructor Thomas "Speedy" Gonzalez wrote about the proper application of J-B in the Brownells GunTech section at www.brownells.com/.aspx/lid=12950/ guntechdetail/Benchrest_Shooting. He recommends forming a J-B infused patch onto a jag into a shape resembling a rifling button. As excerpted from the article:

Most methods of cleaning with J-B Bore Paste such as a patch over a jag or a patch over a brush address the tops of the rifling and the center of the grooves but leave the area where the groove meets the rifling untouched. . . . We want to mimic the rifling button to fill 360 degrees of the bore and groove of our barrel so as not to leave a single spot where carbon fouling can hide.

TOOLS & SUPPLIES:

1) J-B Bore Paste. 2) Bore Guide. 3) Cleaning Rod: A good coated one-piece rod with a ball-bearing handle [such as a **#36 Dewey (749-004-396WS, $31)**] works great. Do not use a stainless or jointed rod! 4) Parker-Hale Brass Jag. 5) High-quality square-cotton patches. The largest patch that will enter the bore is best. 6) Solvent: A good bore solvent such as Butches Bore Shine. 7) Bore Seasoning: Colloidal graphite in a suspension media or LOCK-EEZ purchased from Brownells or most NAPA Auto parts.

Coat the upper third of the patch with J-B Bore Paste. This acts as an adhesive to hold the first fold together. Lay the Parker-Hale style jag about one-quarter of the way over from the left side of the patch. Now fold the patch down over the jag. Liberally coat the remainder of the back of the patch with J-B. This second coating will further bind the patch. Wrap to mimic the rifling button. Add another coat of J-B Bore Paste.

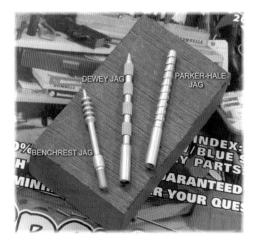

The squarish Parker-Hale Brass Jag at right provides the best shape for the J-B patch. All patching photos courtesy of Thomas "Speedy" Gonzalez.

Coating the upper one-third of the patch with J-B acts as an adhesive.

With the jag on the left side of the patch, fold the patch down over the jag. Liberally coat the remainder of the back of the patch with J-B.

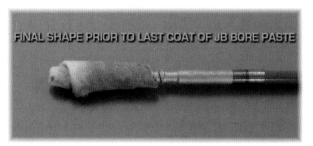

FINAL SHAPE PRIOR TO LAST COAT OF JB BORE PASTE

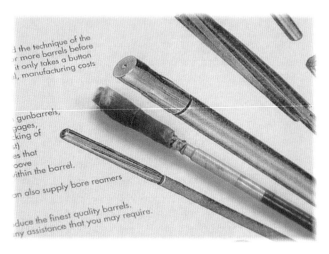

This is the shape you're looking for. It mimics a bullet button, as in the illustration. For more detailed step-by-step directions on the final folding procedure, consult the online article.

Insert your bore guide. Using a different jag, run a clean patch of solvent through the bore. Once there is solvent in the bore, change to the J-B jag and slowly push the wrapped jag through it until you feel the jag and patch contact the throat of the barrel. Since right-hand twist rifling is typical on most rifle barrels, grasp the cleaning rod body firmly and turn it to the right as you apply forward pressure to the rod. This will cause the J-B Bore Paste wrapped patch and jag to engage the rifling and follow the helix of the bore. Once engaged, stop and mark your rod with a silver Sharpie pen or a small band of masking tape to see where the patch is engaging the rifling. Don't pull the wrapped jag beyond that point.

Very slowly and carefully begin to push the rod in and out, working only the first 8 to 10 inches of the barrel for 15 to 30 strokes depending on the condition of the barrel. These 8 to 10 inches are typically where the greatest amount of fouling takes place. After that, gradually increase the length of stroke starting from the witness mark on the rod. When you finally reach the muzzle, carefully push out the patch and unwrap it from the jag. Then slowly withdraw the jag, being careful not to ding the crown with the serrations on the Parker-Hale jag.

Run several wet patches slowly through the bore to remove all of the J-B Bore Paste. Make sure that you run a chamber swab into the chamber to ensure you have removed all J-B Bore Paste from that area. Finish by coating the bore with LOCK-EEZ.

The soft J-B paste liquefies as you use it in rifle, pistol, and shotgun bores, easily removing copper fouling and burned-in moly coatings that can create a cleaning nightmare.

One application of Dyna-Bore Coat will last the useful life of the bore. The 1-fluid-ounce bottle contains enough Dyna-Bore Coat product to treat the bores of five to six long guns.

ing from shotgun bores, restoring pattern density and point of impact quickly and easily.

The **#37 Dyna-Tek Coatings Dyna-Bore Coat Kit (100-006-145WB, $45)** is an advanced chemical treatment that bonds to your gun's barrel walls and produces a permanent, significant reduction in fouling. The result: you can shoot long strings without cleaning, and when you do clean, the carbon, lead, copper, and other fouling come out fast and easy.

The Dyna-Bore Coat Kit is easy to use. Get the bore completely clean following instructions included with the kit, apply the provided alcohol prep solution, and then apply the Bore Coat solution using a loose-fitting patch. To cure it after drying, fire eight to ten rounds. Dyna-Bore bonds molecularly to the barrel and is only .25 microns thick.

The coating has no effect on velocity, point of impact, or group size. But when you clean a typical rifle, you may need as little as three wet patches and three dry patches to get the bore clean, even after firing as many as 800 rounds. You no longer will need to scrub with bronze and stainless-steel brushes or use harsh copper- and lead-removing solvents. In black powder guns, Dyna-Bore Coat eliminates carbon ring buildup. In shotguns, wad residue practically disappears.

The **#38 Brownells Xtreme Air (080-000-809WB, $10)** 10-ounce aerosol canister is the touch-free way to clear dirt, dust, and debris out of hard-to-reach places. The plastic nozzle tube directs a powerful blast of compressed air whenever you need it. It blows grit, dirt, dust, powder residue, and other debris out of hard-to-reach gun surfaces. Squeezing the trigger blasts loose gunk or excess cleaning solvent from actions, trigger assemblies, magazines, gas ports, choke tubes, and shotgun pump mechanisms. Or use it to remove dust and lint from your concealed carry handgun.

The handy canister also makes hundreds of jobs easier at the workbench—or anywhere—with no need for an expensive air compressor. Keep Xtreme Air in your range bag for quick cleanup jobs at the range. And it's great for general-purpose cleaning of your bench, work surfaces, machinery, and computer keyboard.

#39 Dicropan IM (082-008-016WB, $41) is a multi-purpose bluing solution for the gun owner who has just one gun or part to blue. The finish is a beautiful, professional, blue-black color that's sure to please you. The process is easy and simple to do, and the equipment required is minimal.

Dicropan IM has been in the Brownells catalog for years. It is a solution that makes an accelerated rust bluing process possible, and Brownells provides a full set of instructions for this application. The process requires

The Xtreme Air's dry, sterile formula won't leave behind corrosion-inducing moisture, so it's safe for use on all gun metals.

removing finishes or rust from the part, with rust and blue remover. The bare metal is then prepped by polishing, sanding, draw filing, or a combination of all three. It all depends on the condition of the part and type of finish you want on the finished gun.

The instructions then call for heating the part in boiling water, applying the solution and then removing the oxidation that forms on the part with steel wool or a soft wire brush. The process of reheating the part in the boiling water and carding off the oxidation is then repeated until you achieve the depth of color you want.

As presented in the Brownells instructions, the process is as foolproof as it can be. It is safe for use on old, soft-soldered doubles and will give you a very durable and beautiful finish.

An alternative method is to perform the first steps of removing the old bluing and rust and polishing the part as you normally would, as the instructions call for. Instead of a boiling-water bath, use a heat gun. Hang the barrel or any large part over the bench, or hold small parts with a pair of pliers. Then heat the part with the electric hot-air gun until it is hot enough for the IM solution to evaporate as soon as it is applied. It is not critical that the temperature be exact.

Apply the Dicropan IM using a cloth or swab saturated in the solution. If the IM does not evaporate immediately, simply reheat the part until it does.

Most firearms parts require from five to ten coats of IM, but some alloys take 10–15. Hobbyists using this method can have the barrels of a double done in about 45 minutes to an hour and have done an entire Colt 1903 (slide, frame, grip safety, magazine release, and slide lock) in an afternoon.

A coating of rust will form on the part. Using insulated rubber gloves (remember the part is hot!), remove the part from the hangers, take it to the buffer, and wire-brush the entire part, removing the rust. Hang the part back up, heat it and apply a second coat of IM. This process is repeated until you achieve the depth of color you want.

It's really as simple as that! No muss, no fuss, no bother. The quality of the finish depends more on the prep work than the actual bluing. And tough? You bet it's tough! You have been removing the oxidation with a wire wheel or steel wool, so the only way you're going to scratch it is with a sharp piece of steel. Think about it—real rust bluing right in your garage. No need for tanks, burners, highly caustic solutions, or chemicals that you will have to dispose of one day.

Hot-salts bluing is necessary for high-volume shops where time is money and there is plenty of bluing work to be done. But with the heat-gun method and Dicropan IM, now the hobbyist can take care of his own projects with a couple of hours work. Personally, I think that is a breakthrough.

Paul Mazan contributed to this section.

The **#40 Brownells Micro Drop Pinpoint Oiler (080-000-733WB, $20)** fits in your pocket and goes anywhere, so you'll always be prepared when your weapon needs a little lube at the range or in the field.

The bottom cap unscrews to reveal the 2-inch long syringe for pinpoint application of a precise amount of oil. An internal micro plunger controlled by the pushbutton on the top of the oiler acts like a mini-hydraulic system to ensure even flowing, no-squirt, no-drip application.

The Pinpoint Oiler has a rugged all-aluminum construction. O-rings safety seal the oil inside the brushed matte-finish case, which is 5 ¾ inches long and about ⁹⁄₁₀ inch in diameter. A clip secures the Oiler in a pocket.

To refill the applicator, unscrew the knurled end cap and pour in up to 18ccs of the lubricant of your choice, such as Brownells Friction Defense Xtreme Gun Oil, available separately.

Friction Defense Xtreme Gun Oil is sold in 2-ounce and 4-ounce flip-open dropper-tops and a 4-ounce spray can. The blend is one of the most advanced synthetic oils, with water-displacing additives to combat rust caused by moisture and the contaminants in fingerprints.

Brownells' customers liked the company's **#41 Friction Defense Xtreme Gun Oil Aerosol (083-000-043WB, $12)** in bottles so much that the company decided to offer it in an aerosol spray as well. Brownells' Gun Techs call it "slicky"—slick lubrication, plus a sticky quality that keeps Friction Defense Xtreme on metal parts through high-volume shooting sessions.

Friction Defense delivers twice the lubricity of the original Friction Defense formula, with even better corrosion protection and tolerance for extreme operating temperatures. Friction Defense stays slick at temperatures as low as −100° and up to +550°. That makes it suitable for a range of full-auto, semi-auto, or single-shot pistols, rifles, and shotguns.

Micro-fine particles of PTFE, the same material used on non-stick cookware, won't settle in the bottle, and PTFE provides outstanding lubrication on the hottest-running guns. This protection also inhibits the formation of carbon and other fouling byproducts, so guns clean up more quickly and easily than with ordinary petroleum-based oils.

The **#42 Sportsman's Bench Products Vibra-Tite Sportsman's 6-Pack (749-012-643WB, $20)** contains adhesives, thread-locking gels, and lubricants perfect for use on the bench, at the range, or around the house.

In the pack is a half-ounce squeeze tube of Vibra-Tite Drivegrip and Anti Cam-Out fluid, which bonds any fastener and a corresponding tool, making it easier to remove tight screws with worn heads. It's also great for adding integrity to worn adjustable wrenches.

Vibra-Tite Instant Superglue is a clear liquid adhesive perfect for quick repairs. Packaged in a half-ounce resealable bottle, Instant Superglue repairs

The Sportsman's Bench Products Vibra-Tite Sportsman's 6-Pack contains Drivegrip and Anti Cam-Out adhesive, Instant Superglue, Threadlocker Gel Permanent Strength, Threadlocker Gel Medium Strength, and VC-3 Threadmate. Rounding out the 6-pack is a ¼-ounce tube of Vibra-Tite Anti-Seize Compound.

chips on clear surfaces, strengthens cracked wood stocks, and bonds vinyl, rubber, plastic, and laminates.

There are three thread-locking gels in the pack. Vibra-Tite Thread-locker Gel Permanent Strength comes in a ¼-ounce tube. This red gel is recommended for fasteners up to 1-inch in diameter, and as the name suggests, this adhesive permanently locks fasteners it's applied to. Vibra-Tite Threadlocker Gel Medium Strength is a medium-strength blue adhesive that keeps ¼-inch to ¾-inch diameter fasteners from loosening due to vibrations. Packaged in a ¼-ounce tube, this Threadlocker is removable. Vibra-Tite VC-3 Threadmate, available in a ³⁄₁₆-ounce tube, likewise prevents fasteners from loosening due to vibration, but it's easier to remove. Adjust the amount of adhesion you want by varying how much you apply to fasteners on the bench, in the shop, or around the house.

Rounding out the 6-pack is a ¼-ounce tube of Vibra-Tite Anti-Seize Compound. This nickel-graphite lubricant acts as a protective barrier between metals to prevent wear, stop galling, and eliminate seizing due to hot or cold conditions.

Over the years, I've found I prefer more grip than most guns offer out of the box, but I haven't wanted to modify them permanently. Solution: **#43 Brownells "Insta Grip" Non-slip, Adhesive-backed Tape (084-093-000WB, $32)**. It provides additional gripping surface when applied to any firearm. I've added pieces to rifle and shotgun forearms, pistol and revolver grip frames, slides on handguns, and revolver grips.

The issue of grip texture is a personal one. Many, if not most, pistol straps are textured in some way—cut-checking in 20- to 30-lines-per-inch

Medium-texture tape like on the blue gun is best for most uses, but especially in areas that can provide a lot of friction. The more aggressive texture of the heavier grain can rub your fingers raw if it's put in a high-traffic area.

density, molded-in serrations, knurling, and other textures. The various patterns help the shooter control the pistol during recoil. Slick grip panels and straps, as well as unpatterned slides, can make a defensive handgun harder to operate.

The Springfield XD-40 pictured has a variety of built-in textures designed to help the operator use the pistol effectively. There are serrations (arrows) on the trigger-guard front, the front strap, and the rear of the slide, as well as the backstrap. Despite these features, the gun was slick and difficult to rack. To solve that problem, I added a half-inch patch on both sides of the front of the slide roughly where the XD logo appears.

S&W 686-2 wooden grip

Grip panels on the S&W 686-2 357 Magnum offer some traction, but tape on the smooth areas vastly improves grip.

Spots on a Springfield XD-40 40 S&W to consider adding tape to.

The Ruger LCP 380 ACP's frontstrap is a prime area to add tape.

The ATI 1911 Commander 45 ACP's smooth frontstrap offers better control with smooth-grained tape.

On other handguns, such as the Ruger LCP 380 ACP shown nearby, the front strap is serrated but it's still slick. The front strap on the Commander-size ATI 1911, a budget 45 ACP pistol, is smooth, probably to keep the cost down.

The wooden grip on an S&W 686-2 has some side-panel checkering, but the bulk of the grip is slick. Often, such guns, designed to ride in a pants or jacket pocket, have minimalist sights and texturing to ensure they can be retrieved without grabbing clothing. Once drawn, however, they're still slick as eels, and even the Kurz round can make the gun move around in my hand.

Applying the tape is straightforward, as is shown on the slide of the blue safety gun.

Cut the tape to the desired shape with a pair of heavy-duty scissors. Place the Insta-Grip tape on the firearm and check the fit. Don't peel and stick the tape until you've checked the fit. Make sure the tape lays flat and has enough surface area to adhere to.

Then degrease and clean the area of any oils, moisture, or contaminants that will keep the tape from sticking. After cleaning the area to be covered, peel the backing paper from one edge of the Insta-Grip and locate the piece by pressing only the exposed edge of the tape onto the area with finger pressure. Closely observe the location of the tape and adjust the location as necessary. If the location is acceptable, remove the rest of the paper backing and press the tape down with firm finger pressure.

Tip: Take care when using solvents to degrease gun stocks. Some stock finishes (e.g., linseed oil base stock finishes) are not resistant to most solvents. If possible, test the solvent on a small area of the gunstock that will not be noticed (i.e. under the recoil pad or grip cap).

Tip: If you want to place a piece on the front strap of a 1911, cut the strip so that extends under the grips. When the grips are screwed down, they'll lock the strip in place even more firmly than the adhesive will.

CHAPTER THREE

AR-15/M16 GADGETS

B ecause of the modular nature of the AR-15, the rifle lends itself to more tinkering than any other design, except, perhaps, for the Ruger 10-22 small-bore rifle and the 1911 .45 ACP pistol. Chapter 3 covers some of the parts you should consider adding to your Modern Sporting Rifle.

I've touched on some parts and kits for the AR-15 already: #6 AR-15 M16 Action Block and #7 Lower Receiver Vise Block Set 080-000-659WB; the #15 AR-15 Field Parts Kit 078-060-015WB; #18 AR-15 Multi-Tool by DPMS 231-000-007; #28 Otis AR-15 Grip Cleaning Kit 668-000-005; #29 Brownells AR-15/M16 Professional Cleaning System 080-000-573; and the #30 AR-15/M16 Deluxe Buttstock Cleaning Kit 084-000-233WB. You'll use some of them in this chapter.

One way to make over an entire rifle quickly is to install the components in **#44 Brownells DIY Magpul MOE AR-15/M16 Upgrades (080-000-913WB Commercial or 080-000-916 Mil-Spec, $200)**. The Brownells Do-It-Yourself Kit is a handy package of Magpul Original Equipment parts. Those parts and included tools make improving your AR-15 or M16 with Commercial or Mil-Spec buffer tubes a breeze.

The two kits have four common black Magpul parts: Two-Piece Carbine Handguard (100-004-152), AR-15 Standard MOE Pistol Grip (100-003-515), Mag417-Moe Trigger Guard (100-004-156), and a Vertical Front Grip (100-005-588). The fifth MOE part in each kit is a collapsible stock. The stock in the Mil-Spec Kit (100-003-535) fits a 1.15-inch diameter buffer tube. The stock in the Commercial Kit (100-003-538) fits a 1.17-inch diameter buffer tube. To see which buffer tube your rifle requires, use a micrometer to measure the cross-section of your rifle's tube.

To install the parts quickly and easily, Brownells assembled four helpful tools: the **#45 AR-15 Handguard Removal Tool (080-000-487WB, $20)**, **#46 Roll Pin Punch Kit For AR-15/M16 (230-112-105WB, $20)**, **#47 1"**

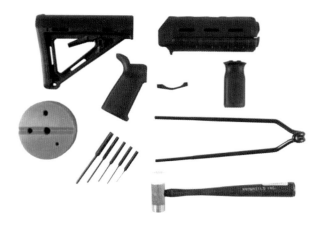

Clockwise from top left, the parts in the #44 Brownells DIY Magpul MOE AR-15/M16 Upgrade Kit (080-000-913) include either a Commercial (100-003-538) or Mil-Spec (100-003-535) stock, Two-Piece Carbine Handguard (100-004-152), Mag417-Moe Trigger Guard (100-004-156), Vertical Front Grip (100-005-588), #45 AR-15 Handguard Removal Tool (080-000-487), #47 1-inch Nylon/Brass Hammer Combo (818-600-100), #46 Roll Pin Punch Kit For AR-15/M16 (230-112-105), #48 Green Rifle Bench Block (080-000-492), and the AR-15 Standard MOE Pistol Grip (100-003-515).

Nylon/Brass Hammer Combo (818-600-100WB, $20), and the **#48 Green Rifle Bench Block (080-000-492WB, $19)**.

These replacement parts address issues with the original military parts, like a slippery and rough pistol grip and the loose rattling of the military-style telescoping buttstock. And they don't require permanent modification or complex disassembly of your rifle.

The Magpul Original Equipment carbine buttstock provides the quality, durability, and ergonomic benefits of Magpul's CTR stock in a drop-in package. Its strong A-frame design is lightweight and comfortable. Yet it provides the operator with plenty of support because the comb contour is wider than a standard-issue M4 stock. And on the butt, a soft synthetic-rubber pad reduces slippage. To improve the stock's fit, a heavy-duty spring-loaded release lever allows fast length-of-pull adjustments. And it won't dig into your hand. For easy carry, the operator will find two slots for web slings and a hole for a toe-mounted sling swivel or clip-on sling. Also, the stock's streamlined exterior and protected release lever won't snag on clothing, gear, a vehicle interior, or vegetation. The buffer tube, carbine buffer, receiver extension nut, and carbine-length action spring are not included.

Roll Pin Punch Kit For
AR-15/M16 (230-112-
105).

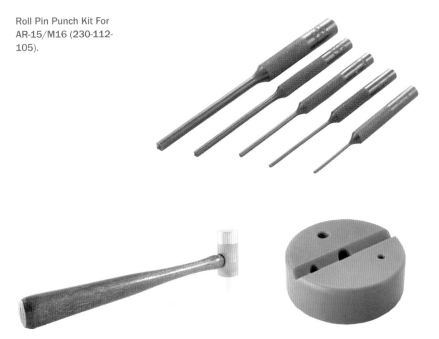

Nylon/Brass Hammer Combo (818-600-100).   Green Rifle Bench Block (080-000-492).

To complement the buttstock, the Magpul AR-15 MOE Grip is a durable, easy-to-install replacement for the factory pistol grip. The one-piece grip is made from the same reinforced high-impact polymer as Magpul's Mission Adaptable MIAD grip. The MOE grip in the kit has crackle texture on the sides and deep horizontal grooves on the front strap and blackstrap. A curved beavertail fills the grip-to-receiver junction. This helps you maintain a comfortable hold and protects the web of your hand.

Adjacent to the grip is a drop-in Mag417 enhanced trigger guard. Its shallow "V" shape provides extra clearance for a shooter wearing gloves. It also eliminates the gap at the rear of the USGI trigger guard, which can trap or pinch your finger. The trigger guard is made of reinforced polymer. Its smooth, contoured surface and rounded edges protect the trigger finger from abrasion. It won't snag on the operator's glove, impeding trigger function. It replaces the factory guard in minutes and requires no permanent alterations to the receiver. You can reinstall the original guard at any time.

The supplied Magpul Two-Piece Carbine Handguard fits onto your standard military service rifle. It takes the place of the round-plastic or older-style triangular hand guards without any modifications to the rifle. By simply pulling back on the Delta ring with the Handguard tool, you can remove the

Brownells AR-15 Handguard Removal
Tool 080-000-487

old hand guards in under a minute and replace them with the two-piece snap-on MOE hand guards. Use MOE-compatible attachments to outfit your rifle with accessories. Horizontal slots at the two, six, and ten o'clock positions let you install bolt-on accessory rails or an MOE Illumination Kit, available separately, exactly where you want to mount your accessories. The Magpul hand guards don't require any modifications, and you don't have to remove other parts of your rifle. The guard's trapezoidal cross-section and ridges on the underside help the operator maintain a secure grip for better control. An integral aluminum heat shield protects the shooter's hand from a hot barrel. Side extensions and a pronounced lip at the front prevent the forward hand from slipping onto a hot gas block.

The final upgrade part is the Magpul Vertical Grip. This lightweight grip positions your support hand close to the barrel to help you maintain maximum weapon control. The ergonomically shaped design is optimized for use with the "thumb break" method of grasping the weapon. Yet it works just as well with a traditional vertical-grip handhold. It is designed to clamp easily onto Magpul MOE and Bushmaster Adaptive Combat Rifle hand guards without an accessory rail.

The tool kit for this package includes the polyethylene Brownells Bench Block. It provides a stable surface when driving pins out of an action. The center V-groove keeps cylindrical parts steady so they won't roll. The extra size and weight make the block stable on your bench. The block can be drilled or modified with hand tools. It will not melt when machined.

To make short work of the Magpul Handguard installation, the included Brownells AR-15 Handguard Removal Tool eliminates the need for a second pair of hands when removing AR-type hand guards. Simply insert the hooked end of the tool into the mag well, position the handles over the Delta ring, and push down to compress the delta ring spring. It's made of strong ¼-inch steel rod, and the synthetic rubber coating won't scratch your rifle.

Driving out and then reinstalling the trigger-guard pins is easy with the Roll Pin Punch Kit For AR-15s and M16s. Made by Mayhew Steel for Brownells, the included punches properly install or remove roll pins without damaging the pin or the surrounding metal. A small raised projection in the face of the punch automatically centers the punch and prevents the roll pin from collapsing.

You don't want to scratch or scuff your rifle during the trigger-installation process, which the 1-Inch Nylon/Brass Hammer Combo prevents. The nylon head resists breaking and won't mar metal if you have to tap a part into place. The solid-brass head provides the right force when driving punches in or out.

To begin the installation, first ensure your AR is unloaded. At this point, it's also a good idea to unload all your magazines and remove all live ammunition from the disassembly area, and put on safety glasses. Point the rifle in a safe direction, press in on the magazine catch, and remove the magazine.

With your finger off the trigger and out of the trigger guard, lock the action open. Once the action is locked to the rear, both visually and physically inspect the chamber and the magazine well to be sure that no ammunition remains in either place.

Now, let's look at the buttstock installation. There are two types of carbine receiver extensions, informally called buffer tubes: Mil-Spec and Commercial. Before proceeding, confirm you have the correct MOE stock for your receiver extension. Incorrect installation will result in damage to your stock and or tube. The easiest way to distinguish between Mil-Spec and Commercial receiver extensions is to measure the tube diameter. Mil-Spec receiver extensions have a slightly smaller diameter of approximately 1.15 inches. They also usually have a flat back. Both the correct Mil-Spec MOE stock and the Commercial MOE stock will fit over the Mil-Spec tube, but the Commercial version will be noticeably looser. If you have a rare Mil-Spec tube with a slanted back, you also need an extended butt pad, available separately.

Commercial receiver extensions like the one on this gun have a slightly larger diameter of about 1.17 inches and usually have slanted backs. Some Commercial tubes may have a flat back and will still be compatible. Only the

Commercial MOE will slide easily over a Commercial buffer tube. Do not try to force a Mil-Spec MOE over the larger Commercial tube. Also, most Commercial receiver extension tubes are longer than standard Mil-Spec tubes, and often have a slanted back. All Commercial tubes with slanted backs require the use of the Extended Buttpad, which is already included with the Commercial MOE buttstock.

After verifying that you have the correct MOE version for your buffer tube, remove the existing stock. Then, to install the MOE stock, gently mate the stock body with the carbine receiver extension and slide them together until the stock stops just over two inches in. Depress the release latch with one hand. With the other hand, grasp both ends of the release pin and pull down firmly. If the pin is stiff, you may need hard, flat-edge objects to push the pin ends down.

When the pins move downward, push the stock forward to complete the mount. To adjust the length of the stock, fully depress the release latch and pull the stock rearward to extend it. Push the stock forward to collapse it. Partially depressing the release latch and moving the stock to the desired position allows you to select intermediate positions.

To remove the stock, pull it all the way to the rear. Depress the release latch with one hand. With the other hand, grasp both ends of the release pin and pull down firmly and pull the stock free of the tube.

To install the Carbine Handguards and MVG grip, first use the Brownells forearm removal tool to take off the existing forearm sections. Seat the tip of tool in the magazine well and use the tool extensions to grip and apply pressure on delta ring toward the receiver. Remove the factory hand guards, but leave the tool in place.

Orient the new Magpul hand guards with the thinner triangular piece on top and the wider ribbed grip with metal heat shield on the bottom. The lip on the bottom grip should be forward. The barrel-nut notches on both hand guards should be toward the rear.

Before installing the new hand guards on the rifle, put the MVG front grip on the bottom guard. There are three slots on the bottom guard that will accept the indexing points on the grip. When the MVG is in the right spot, install the 10-24 socket head screw and washer through the bottom then the hole in the MVG.

Thread the weld nut onto the 10-24 socket head screw and hand tighten using a ⅛-inch hex key or a ⅛-inch magnetized hex bit in the Magna-Tip handle. Install the new two-piece hand guards, using the Handguard tool to compress delta ring.

Snap the front part of the bottom Handguard and front grip combo in first, then press it in toward the Delta ring while you squeeze the tool extension to exert pressure on the ring and compress it. Snap the bottom guard in place, and release tension on the tool. Grab the top guard and snap the front in, then squeeze the tool again to compress the delta ring. Snap the back into place and remove the tool.

Next, assemble the Standard Pistol Grip. To install the pistol grip, you'll need a large flathead screwdriver with a shaft at least 3 ½ inches in length, and the Brownells bench block. I recommend using the Brownells #13 Magna-Tip Ratchet Handle and magnetic bits. To stabilize the action, use the #7 Lower Receiver Vise Block or place the receiver onto the supplied bench block with the grip facing upward. Remove the standard grip by unscrewing the grip screw and sliding the grip off the receiver.

Capture the detent spring during removal. While you have it out, apply a bit of grease to the spring. The grease will lubricate the spring and trap it in the grip during installation. Insert the detent spring into the Magpul MOE grip. Slip the MOE grip onto the grip frame.

Add a little grease to the grip screw threads. Capture the screw slot on the magnetic bit. If you don't have a Magna-Tip bit and handle, apply masking tape to the screwdriver tip to hold the screw. Insert the screw into the grip and tighten the screw. Then install the grip plug.

To install the new MOE trigger guard, keep the rifle in the #7 Vise Block or set the rifle upside down on the bench block and remove the existing trigger guard. Using a ⅛-inch punch from the Upgrade Kit, depress the front detent spring and rotate the trigger guard down, clear of the receiver. Using the same punch, use the nylon-brass combo hammer to tap out the rear roll pin and remove the trigger guard.

The roll pin punch set included in the Upgrade Kit is specially designed to remove these pins without damaging the receiver, but take care nonetheless. Place the MOE trigger guard into the receiver with the Magpul logo down and the smaller cutout forward on the receiver. Check the fit and hole alignment.

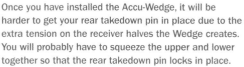

Once you have installed the Accu-Wedge, it will be harder to get your rear takedown pin in place due to the extra tension on the receiver halves the Wedge creates. You will probably have to squeeze the upper and lower together so that the rear takedown pin locks in place.

While supporting the underside of the trigger guard, verify the hole alignment and carefully drive in the rear roll pin using the ⅛-inch punch and nylon hammer. Using a ¹⁄₁₆-inch hex key, slowly hand-tighten the front set screw until it is flush with the receiver tab. Don't over tighten.

Perform a function check to ensure all the parts are installed properly.

The **#49 Brownells AR-15/M16 Accu-Wedge (080-000-663WB, $5)** is one of the fastest, easiest, cheapest accuracy improvements you'll ever find for your AR. The tough, high-density synthetic-rubber wedge drops into the space behind the takedown pin in the lower receiver to provide tension between the receiver halves and prevent movement for improved accuracy. It can be trimmed to accommodate any variation in upper-to-lower receiver fit.

The **#50 AR-15/M16 T-Grip Vertical Forend Grip (100-003-846WB, $90)** by the Mako Group has a unique shape that gives the AR-15 shooter an exceptionally solid and comfortable grasp on the rifle. The T-Grip is narrow at the top and has a comfortable palm swell, finger grooves, and stippled texturing. These features improve how your AR or M16 points, and during rapid-fire strings, a better grip means better recoil control and improved targeting.

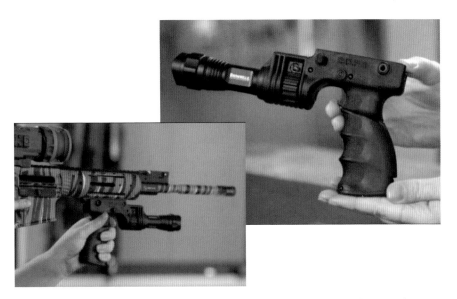

The T-Grip clamps securely to any Picatinny or Weaver-style rail, and a quick-release pushbutton lock allows fast installation and removal. An additional locking bolt provides extra-secure mounting. A trapdoor in the bottom hides a roomy storage compartment.

A screw-tightened collar securely retains any handheld tactical flashlight with a 1-inch diameter body.

A convenient trigger mechanism operates most pushbutton end-cap switches, so the operator can activate the light without breaking his grip. A master on/off switch locks out the trigger to prevent accidental activation.

The **#51 AR-15/M16 Oversized Charging Handle Latch (080-000-758WB, $18)** has an extra-large, deeply grooved finger pad for positive contact that helps you charge the rifle quickly under stress. Made from extra-strong 4340 chrome-moly steel hardened to Rc 38-45, the latch has a tough manganese-phosphate Parkerized finish for added surface strength and corrosion resistance. It fits Mil-Spec AR-15/M16 charging handles.

To install, you will need a 4-ounce to 8-ounce ball-peen hammer and a $\frac{3}{32}$ roll pin punch or starter punch and roll pin holder or the #46 Roll Pin Punch Kit For AR-15/M16 230-112-105 to replace your existing latch. Use the #48 Green Rifle Bench Block 080-000-492 to capture the roll pin you remove, as it is easily lost.

Place the charging handle flat on the bench vise and use the roll-pin punch to drive out the pivot pin into the bench block. Remove the latch while

AR-15/M16 Oversized
Charging Handle Latch
080-000-758WB.

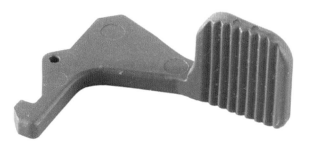

The pad angles out 90 degrees from the receiver so you can slap at the latch and get a secure grasp, even with gloves.

making sure the spring is controlled or maintained. The spring will usually remain in the handle and may not be visible while it is still in position.

Slide the Brownells Oversize Latch into the slot with the textured surface to the front. Align the pivot hole with the rollpin hole in the handle and use the roll pin holder to start the roll pin into the hole. Do not use much force, as the handle will have minimal friction on the pin and the latch should rotate on the pin and will have only a small amount of friction on the installed pin.

Drive the pin in flush with the body of the handle so it clears the upper receiver slot on the top and bottom. The pin should be replaced if it is bent or has been damaged during disassembly or reassembly. Check for proper movement of the latch and to make sure it is under some spring tension before installation into the rifle.

The **#52 AR-15/M16 C-Mag by The Beta Company (100-003-387WB, $290)** is a 100-round dual drum magazine that's great for extended shooting, allowing you to spend more time shooting and less time changing mags.

The C-Mag's polymer composite body is available in solid black or black with a clear drum face so you can see how much ammo is left. Unloaded, the C-Mag weighs 2¼ pounds.

Some shooters might worry that carrying 100 rounds under their ARs would make the rifles cumbersome or awkward to shoot. But the C-Mag's even weight distribution keeps your rifle well balanced and nimble.

The C-Mag comes with a tool that speeds loading—simply push five rounds at a time into the interlinking straight clip to automatically double stack and alternately load both drums.

A double-stitched, nylon carry case attaches to your web belt and includes individual compartments for the magazine, loading tool, and graphite tubes. Because the hardware is steel and the feed rails are aluminum, the C-Mag will provide years of reliable service. Also included are two tubes of graphite lubricant for optimal feeding, plus a snap-on synthetic cover to keep dirt from entering the follower end of the magazine.

The **#53 Striplula AR-15 Magazine Loader (100-003-330WB, $30)** and **#54 Striplula Ruger Mini-14 Magazine Loader (593-000-048WB, $33)** make inserting 5.56mm or 223 Remington rounds in your AR-15, M16, and Ruger Mini-14 magazines fast and painless. Made by Maglula, Ltd., the polymer Striplula device is constructed of durable, reinforced polymer for dependable operation under extreme field conditions.

Striplula Ruger Mini-14
Magazine Loader
593-000-048WB.

Striplula AR-15 Magazine Loader 100-003-330WB.

To use, attach the Striplula to the top of a magazine, insert a 10-round stripper clip or loose rounds, fold down the top handle, and press the cartridges into the magazine. With stripper clips, you can load a 20-round magazine in less than eight seconds. The ambidextrous, grooved thumb slide provides a non-slip grip for right- or left-hand loading. Also, you can use the Striplula to unload a 20-round magazine in ten seconds.

The **#55 AR-15 M16 B.A.D. Lever by Magpul (100-004-755WB, $30)** allows the rifle shooter to release the bolt with the trigger finger, keeping his hand in the ready position on the pistol grip.

The Magpul Battery Assist Device, or B.A.D., is an extended bolt release. It streamlines bolt-catch manipulation to get the weapon into battery more quickly. The trigger finger can stay outside the trigger guard as you

The Magpul Battery Assist Device is made of a high-grade aluminum alloy. It's hardcoat anodized to a Type III, Class 2 Mil-Spec for extra strength and wear resistance.

operate the lever. The factory bolt catch retains normal function with the B.A.D. installed.

It's easy to install and remove, with no rifle disassembly required. The B.A.D. lever clamps securely to the factory bolt release with a Torx-head screw and extends a paddle through the front of the trigger guard to the right-hand side of the weapon.

Battle Arms Development, Inc. is an American-owned small business that makes accessories and parts for AR-15, M16, and M4-style rifles. **#56 Ambidextrous Safety Selectors (100-006-839WB, $100)** are one of the company's products.

These oversized, deeply grooved safety levers allow you to use either hand to turn M16-style rifles on and off. The machined, heat-treated Parker-

Brownells sells two versions of the Ambi safeties, one for semi-autos and one for full-auto models.

You can customize the feel by positioning the larger pad on either side of the receiver.

Torx screws and an
L-key wrench for
mounting the safeties
are included.

ized steel safety selector has oversized contact pads on both sides of the receiver for easy ambidextrous operation.

The large surface area lets you manage the safety while wearing gloves, and eliminates fumbling in the dark. Also, the pads' channels provide a secure grip under stress or when your hands are wet.

The **#57 Tritium HK-Style Rear Sight (100-005-085WB, $180)** and **#58 Tritium HK-Style Front Sight (100-005-084WB, $150)** by Troy Industries provide failsafe backup when your primary optic or red-dot sight fails.

The sight bodies flip up easily when you need them. They lock up under powerful spring pressure and two locking detent balls, so they can't accidentally fold down. Also, the rear aperture and front post stand at the same height as factory sights, making integration of these sights on your rifle easy.

To adjust bullet impact, a detent-locking adjustment wheel on the rear sight lets you change the windage setting in ½-MOA increments. The front sight clamps to the Handguard accessory rail on the same plane as flattop and are only ½ inch high when folded. All models have M4-type posts that are elevation adjustable in ½-MOA increments.

The HK-style rear sight has two same-plane round apertures. The large .190-inch aperture provides a wide field of view for close-in targets, while a .070-inch aperture is calibrated for engaging long-range targets. It has a tritium dot on each side of the large aperture. No-snag protective ears shield the apertures from impact. They're low profile as well— .460 inch tall when folded.

You'll notice there are no protruding knobs or levers to catch on brush, clothing, or other equipment. They attach to your rifle's rails with a flat-head screwdriver.

Hidden inside this **#59 AR-15/M16 M4 Buttpad/Monopod (100-005-996WB, $50)** by Mako Group is an integral monopod that deploys instantly, providing support for precise shooting with AR-15, M16, and M4 rifles.

The rubber pad slips onto the butt plate of any M4-type collapsible stock, and if you need it, simply pull on this knob to instantly deploy the monopod.

Four locking detents at three-quarter-inch increments let you set the height up to 3 ¼ inches, while the threaded extension rod can be unscrewed an additional 3 ¾ inches for 7 inches of total elevation.

Adjust the knurled locking ring to keep the anodized aluminum rod in place when it's set. When you're done, hit the pushbutton release to retract it.

The **#60 Geissele Automatics SSA-E Super Semi-Automatic Enhanced Trigger (100-006-357WB, $230)** is a finely tuned semi-automatic-only version of the company's full-auto two-stage combat trigger presently used by U.S Special Operations.

Built on the Geissele (pronounced GUYS-lee) SSA chassis, the SSA-E

On the HK-style front sight, the shooter sees a distinctive "globe" shape that aids in fast target acquisition under stress. A self-illuminating tritium dot on the post allows for precise shot placement in low-light conditions.

The Troy Industries Folding Battle Rear Sights are made in the US of stainless steel and aluminum components and come in Black or Dark Earth finishes.

The 55/8-inch tall, 2 inch wide textured neoprene-rubber pad from Mako Group adds 1 inch to the overall length of stock. It also provides grip to keep the stock seated on the shoulder, and it reduces felt recoil. The entire assembly weighs 10.2 ounces.

provides enhanced trigger control and weapon accuracy while maintaining the robustness and reliability of a combat-proven two-stage trigger.

The Geissele SSA-E is a simple design similar to the original M16 trigger—in fact, the number of parts are identical. Internally, there are no adjustment screws to come loose and all springs are captive, so they can't get lost during disassembly in the field.

The SSA-E's reduced first- and second-stage pull weights result in a trigger with a smooth, light first-stage take-up and a crisp second-stage break. The Geissele SSA-E has a total pull weight of about 3.5 pounds, split between a 2.3 pound first stage and 1.2 pounds on the second stage. The shooter can't adjust pull weights and sear engagement.

The SSA-E is ideal for use in precision rifles where accuracy and reliability are critical. But the Geissele SSA-E trigger also allows the shooter to slap through the trigger pull on close-in shots.

The SSA-E's trigger and hammer are made from quality tool steel cut by a wire electrical discharge machining system for the smoothest surface finish. The hammer and trigger pins are a close

The Geissele SSA-E is a simple design similar to the original M16 trigger.

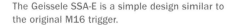

The SSA-E is ideal for use in precision rifles.

The SSA-E's trigger and hammer are made from quality tool steel cut by EDM.

slip fit into nominal receiver holes, so the trigger can be installed and removed with rudimentary tools.

Spending $150 or more for trigger parts on every AR-style rifle you own can turn into big money fast. If you can't justify expensive full triggers in all of your rifles, then the **#61 AR-15 Reduced Power Spring Kit By J P Enterprises (452-000-007WB, $12)** may be for you.

The JP Enterprises custom trigger and hammer springs create a livable 4.5- to 5-pound smooth trigger in a rifle with standard trigger components. The kit includes trigger-return spring, hammer spring, and disconnector spring and complete instructions on how to prep these parts for best results.

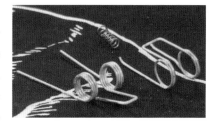

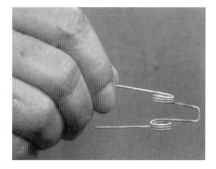

Also included is RyDol sear compound. RyDol contains hexagonal boron nitride and PTFE micron sized particles in suspension. Used according to the preparation instructions, RyDol penetrates the trigger engagement surfaces and produces a super slick, consistent metal finish.

Once you install the JP spring kit, the manufacturer recommends you only shoot US-manufactured domestic ammunition or reloads with domestic non-NATO spec primers.

The **#62 Zel Custom AR-15/M16 Tactilite Bolt-Action Upper Receiver (100-005-531WB, $2050)** combines with any off-the-shelf AR-15 lower to create a professional-quality, ultra-long-range rifle. Buying an upper instead of a complete rifle is cheaper, easier, and gives you a more flexible rifle platform than buying a complete rifle. Also, depending on your state and local regulations, an upper can be shipped directly to you without the time, hassle, and cost of buying a complete rifle. The Tactilite may be the most affordable way to own a rifle chambered for .50 BMG.

The Tactilite is a complete upper assembly. It includes the upper receiver, bolt action, barrel, muzzle brake, and Handguard. It also comes with a heavy-duty hammer and spring, which you can install at your option. Using the illustrated instructions, conversion takes less than five minutes and requires no special tools or skills.

The Tactilite upper receiver starts as a 20-pound piece of steel and ends as a 3.5-pound precision component. The Tactilite features a scope rail that is machined directly in the upper receiver for perfect barrel-alignment and unmatched strength.

All Tactilite models feature a standard free-floating barrel, and they're finished in black CeraKote, one of the most durable and finest looking firearms finishes available. Configured with a Lothar-Walther barrel, the Tactilite upper weighs about fifteen pounds. The button-rifled barrel is available in 4140 or LW19 chrome-moly steel, depending on the model. Fully configured with lower, scope and bipod, it weighs about twenty pounds, depending on the components. Unlike semi-automatic systems, the Tactilite's bolt action puts little stress on the lower. The lower serves primarily as a housing for the trigger group.

The Tactilite is a complete upper assembly, which is an accessory. This means that no license, background check, or federal paperwork is required, so the Tactilite gets shipped straight to the customer. State laws vary on the .50 BMG, so please familiarize yourself with relevant state laws before buying that upper. In particular, California has unusual rules for possessing a .50 BMG, so we suggest that you familiarize yourself with those rules.

The T1 Ultralite is a single shot chambered for the popular .50 BMG cartridge, with a 29-inch Mossberg-made 4140 chrome-moly barrel with USMil-Spec standard chamber. This barrel has 8-groove, 1-in-15-inch-twist rifling, and the total upper's weight is 16.7 pounds with the 29-inch barrel.

The heat-treated 4340 steel bolt uses the time-tested two-lug push-feed design for tremendous strength and reliability.

The 7075 aluminum Handguard has integral MIL-STD 1913 Picatinny quad-rails for mounting a full range of accessories, including a bipod and, on the extended top rail, any optic.

All models feature an integrated muzzle brake for reduced felt recoil and fast follow-up shots.

The $2,550 T2 Ultralite is a .50 BMG repeater with the same features as the T1 and a side-mounted, 5-round Accuracy International magazine. It also has a USMil-Spec standard chamber in barrel lengths of 24 or 29 inches.

CHAPTER 4

HANDGUN GADGETS

Thre are mountains of handgun gadgets that fix, upgrade, or otherwise maximize the utility of sidearms for carry, target shooting, plinking, or other uses.

Shooting a wheelgun is a blast, and improving the function of your revolver can make the experience even better. Brownells has assembled a kit to do just that—upgrade your Smith & Wesson revolver in the areas that count most. The **#63 Brownells Do-It-Yourself S&W J-Frame Revolver Upgrade Kit (080-000-849WB, $90)** includes replacement parts for the grip and springs, the tools needed to install those parts, and a clip draw.

The Pro-Spring Kit For S&W J-Frame Revolver contains three different rate-reduced power rebound springs plus one reduced-power hammer spring. Heavy factory springs inevitably result in a rough and heavy trigger. Carefully choosing the right spring pressure with the kit's 13-, 14-, or 15-pound rebound springs can improve the trigger without compromising function.

The grip is where the rubber hits the road in shooter comfort, and the Hogue Monogrip is a one-piece solution to make your wheelgun handle better. This single-piece rubber grip slides onto the revolver frame from the bottom, requiring no modifications of the firearm. Monogrips not only dress up a gun, they also are designed to provide optimal pointing characteristics.

To make the job simpler, the kit also contains the Brownells Magna-Tip handle with three custom bits for S&W Strain, Windage, Side Plate and Sight attaching screws. These short-shank S&W bits are hollow-ground to transmit all the energy of twist (torque) evenly and smoothly.

The Brownells S&W Rebound Slide Tool is a dedicated tool used to grab and compress the rebound slide spring in Smith & Wesson revolvers. It's specially bent and slotted, and it is really about the only way to get past the frame pin to grab and compress the rebound slide spring. It fits all J, K, L, and N frames, and it won't scratch your valuable J-frame.

The parts in the Brownells Pro Spring Kit For The J-Frame Revolver are, clockwise from lower left, a Hogue 60000 Rubber Monogrip, a Brownells S&W Rebound Slide Tool, a Magna-Tip Screwdriver Handle, a clip draw, replacement springs, and a special collection of S&W Bits.

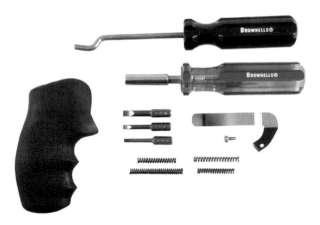

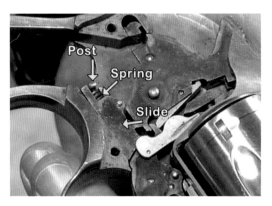

Above: The Brownells S&W Rebound Slide Tool is specially bent and slotted to get at and remove the rebound slide spring.

The kit comes with detailed written instructions. An installation video is available online at Brownells.com.

The **#64 Do-It-Yourself Ruger Mark III Performance Upgrade Kits (080-000-917WB, $150)** contain easy-to-install replacement parts for your pistol's factory trigger and hammer and your choice of stylish Cocobolo grip panels.

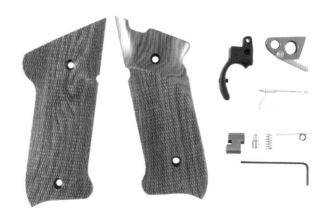

The components in the Do-It-Yourself Ruger Mark III Performance Upgrade Kits include, clockwise from left, Cocobolo grip panels (either right hand or ambi), machined-aluminum target trigger, target hammer with micro-polished sear, and various springs, pins, and tools.

The trigger parts, made by the renowned Volquartsen Custom shop in Iowa, provide a smooth, crisp, 2 ¼-pound trigger pull in your Ruger Mark III, Ruger 22/45 Mark III, or Ruger 22/45 pistol.

The machined-aluminum target trigger has a smooth, radiused .36-inch-wide face that feels great on your trigger finger. It also adjusts for take-up and overtravel with the included Allen wrench. Internally, the redesigned stainless-steel target hammer and micro-polished sear are surface ground to exact tolerances for a short, fast trigger pull. Also, all the engagement surfaces are precision-ground and polished. There's no tedious stoning required.

The perfectly matched polished trigger plunger and trigger-rebound spring further reduce trigger pull and smooth and speed cycling. An extended bolt release completes the trigger package.

While you're upgrading your Mark III's performance, you can also upgrade its looks with new grips made by Majestic Arms. The DIY Ruger Upgrade Kits contain Cocobolo wood grips in two styles to dress up your Ruger pistol. The dark orange-brown Cocobolo wood displays distinct black-grain stripes. The colors are accented by clean, precise 20-lpi checkering.

In one kit, there are right-hand grips with a smooth, comfortable thumb rest for right-handed shooters. The other kit contains ambidextrous grips. They offer a low-profile thumb rest on each panel to accommodate either right- or left-handed shooters.

The **#65 Brownells Do-It-Yourself Glock 17 Sight Upgrade Kit (080-000-919WB, $200)** contains the items you need to easily remove your Glock's factory sights and install tritium night sights in their places. Included in the

The components of the #65 Brownells Do-It-Yourself Glock 17 Sight Upgrade Kit 080-000-919WB are, from left to right, the Ed Brown Glock Front Sight Tool, Meprolight's Tru-Dot Day & Night Sights, and the MGW Precision Glock Rear Sight Adjustment Tool.

Kit are Meprolight's Tru-Dot Day & Night Sights, an Ed Brown Glock Front Sight Tool, and an MGW Precision Glock Rear Sight Adjustment Tool.

These particular Tru-Dots fit on Glock 17s originally equipped with factory non-adjustable sights. There's no switch to turn on and no batteries to wear out. The embedded tritium capsules provide more-accurate aiming in low-light conditions, and NATO, the United States and Israeli armies, and law enforcement have proven their ruggedness.

The Ed Brown Glock Front Sight Tool easily removes and installs Glock front sights. The Brown Tool fits the small hexhead screw that holds Glock front sights in place, and the Brown Tool's shank fits into Magna-Tip screwdriver and ratchet handles.

Replacing rear night sights by hammering them out with a punch can damage the sights' tritium-gas capsules that glow in the dark. MGW's specialized sight-pushing tool fits the Austrian gun's slide and the sides of the Tru-Dot rear sight perfectly, preventing such damage.

A thumbscrew securely locks the slide so it's fully supported in the rigid, machined aluminum body. Separate slots in the screw mechanism

The Ed Brown Glock Front Sight Tool fits over the tiny hexhead screw that holds the front sight.

GLOCK FRONT SIGHT INSTALLATION

1) Slip the Ed Brown Glock Front Sight Tool over the tiny hexhead screw that holds the front sight. You may be able to grasp the Tool's shaft and loosen the screw by hand. If not, then use a Magna-Tip screwdriver handle or Magna-Tip ratchet handle, available separately, for better control. Back the hexhead screw out and remove the front sight.

2) Insert the blade of the Tru-Dot front sight into the oval cutout at the front of the slide. The Tru-Dot blade should fit snugly. Place the hexhead screw into the Ed Brown tool, and put a tiny bit of medium strength threadlocking compound on the screw threads. Start the hexhead screw into the threaded sight shaft, ensuring the screw goes in straight. Tighten until it's snug, but don't overtighten the tiny screw.

3) Check the alignment to make sure the front blade sits flush and square on the slide.

GLOCK REAR SIGHT INSTALLATION

On the polymer rear sight, the Glock's original sight is friction-fit into the dovetail at the rear of the slide. Use the MGW sight tool to remove it.

1) Center the MGW sight-pusher block by rotating the T-handle.

2) Once the sight-pusher block is centered, turn the MGW logo away from you, and insert the bare slide, muzzle pointed away, onto the sleeve at the bottom of the tool. The sleeve is cut specifically for the back of the Glock slide and should fit snugly. Spin the star-knob handle at the bottom of the unit to tighten the slide's position in the tool. Make sure it's very tight and secure.

3) Once the slide is locked in place, ensure that the pusher segment is centered on the sight body. Grip and turn the T-handle to drift the rear sight out from left to right. Turn the handle until the sight can be pulled out of the dovetail with your fingers.

4) Unclamp the slide by loosening the star-knob handle and push the slide back toward you slightly.

5) Insert the Tru-Dot rear sight into the dovetail. Push the slide forward until it is centered in the pusher block. Then drift it right to left into the slide dovetail. If the sight is too tight to start or push, you may have to lightly sand or file the bottom of the sight to accept the new base.

6) Center the sight on the frame, and check its alignment with the new front-sight post and tritium capsule. When you go to the range, take the MGW tool with you to make small horizontal sight changes.

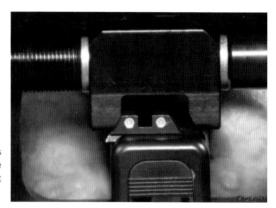

The Glock's factory polymer sight is friction-fit into the dovetail at the rear of the slide. Use the MGW sight tool to remove it.

engage the sight and firmly concentrate screw force to loosen sights from tight dovetails.

The hardened-steel handle provides plenty of leverage, while self-lubricating, oil-impregnated Oilite bronze bearings and extra-fine threads ensure smooth, precise movement.

To begin the sight-replacement process, first ensure your Glock is unloaded and put on safety glasses.

Disassemble your empty and safe Glock down to the slide. Do this by pulling the slide back to release the slide-stop lever, and close the action.

Point the empty pistol in a safe direction, and then pull the trigger. You will hear the firing pin move forward. The trigger must be in the rearmost position to remove the slide.

Hold the pistol in either hand so that four fingers grasp the top of the slide. With these four fingers, pull and hold the slide back about one-tenth of an inch. Simultaneously, pull down and hold both sides of the slide lock, using the thumb and index finger of your free hand. Push the slide forward until it is fully separated from the receiver.

The recoil-spring assembly is under tension and can spring loose, causing eye or other injury. Be sure to control the recoil-spring assembly during the next step.

Push the recoil-spring assembly slightly forward while lifting it away from the barrel. Remove the recoil-spring assembly. Lift the barrel from the slide. Now you can get to the hexhead screw holding the front sight on the underside of the slide.

The #66 Meprolight Universal Sight Installation Tool 387-100-000 has an aluminum body with a hardened steel adjustment screw. It is 6 inch wide, 4 ½ inch high, and weighs 2 pounds.

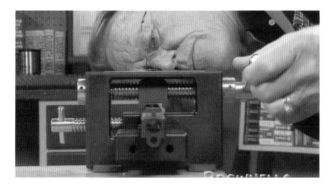

Turn the hardened handle, and the threaded square adjustment screw provides plenty of leverage.

#66 Meprolight's Universal Sight Installation Tool (387-100-000WB, $740) adjusts and installs more than 40 different semi-auto pistol sights, all without damaging the sights or the slides.

The Tool's multi-position slide-support block and separate slide clamp accurately adjusts cross-dovetail pistol sights quickly and precisely. Turn the hardened handle, and the threaded square adjustment screw provides plenty of leverage to move stubborn sights without damaging them.

Machined from a solid block of aluminum alloy, the Universal Tool's body won't flex under stress. If you want to mount it on your bench for better control, use the included attachment ears.

The Tool comes with complete instructions and a pistol-sight reference chart. It won't install tenon-style front sights.

The Uni-Max Laser's matte-black Zytel housing has the strength and durability needed to withstand the shock of rapid-fire recoil. Its compact housing lets it fit in many soft-sided and general fit holsters.

The **#67 Lasermax Uni-Max Micro Rail Mounted Laser (100-006-164WB, $130)** fits nearly any pistol accessory rail, making the super-small laser sight ideal for compact and sub-compact concealed carry pistols. It's only 1 inch long, 1 ⅛ inches wide, and a ½ inch tall. You might not notice it's on the gun, because the Micro weighs just .43 ounces. Even better, it attaches to a carry gun in seconds using a flat-blade screwdriver.

Despite its small size, the Micro projects a powerful red beam powered by a 1/3N lithium battery. The unit's ambidextrous tap on/off switch won't hang up or snag when holstered. A 10-minute time-out feature preserves battery life, for a 5-hour total run time. Point of aim is adjustable for windage and elevation with the included Allen wrench.

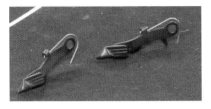

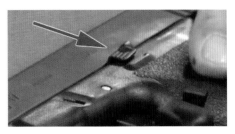

The Extended Lever has a much larger finger pad and a trapezoid-shaped bump that help ensure you release the slide fast, on the first try, after a reload. And don't worry about carry problems. The Extended Lever's low profile and smooth contours will not affect holster fit or snag on clothing.

The **#68 Extended Slide Release Lever for Glocks (100-002-748WB, $12)** is a drop-in replacement for your pistol's factory slide release. The larger raised pad on the Extended Lever makes activating the Glock's slide release easier, rather than having to make multiple swipes on the factory lever to release the slide and chamber the next round.

Separate Extended Slide-Release Lever models fit current-production 3-Pin and early 2-Pin pistols, plus G37, 38, and 39 pistols chambered in 45 GAP. The 3-Pin model fits all guns with separate trigger, locking block, and trigger housing pins, including early 2-Pin G19. The 3-pin does not fit early G17, G17L, and G34 2-Pin guns.

The 2-Pin Extended Slide-Release Lever fits G17s, 17Ls, and 34s that do not have a locking block pin, and which were manufactured from 1986 to mid-2002.

#69 Crimson Trace Laserguards (100-005-026WB, $190) fit below the barrel of many compact polymer-framed handguns, providing accurate, easy-

The Laserguards fit many pistols, including the Kel-Tec P3AT/P32, Kel-Tec PF9, Glock 19, 23, 26, 27, and 36; Ruger LCP, Kahr CW9/CW40/P9/PM9/PM40, S&W Sigma Full Size, Kel-Tec P2AT/P32, even the Pink Ruger LCP.

to-see sighting lasers without adding mass. A tab-and-groove interlocking system securely attaches to the gun's trigger guard, seamlessly integrating with the frame without removing any pins or using any of the firearm's screws.

The Laserguards use CT's smaller 3.3mm-diameter laser diode, which reduces the overall size of the laser diode housing. The various models either use two #357 silver-oxide batteries or a single ⅓ N 3-volt lithium battery, keeping the Laserguard compact yet very powerful.

The Glock Laserguards come with an accessory pack that contains batteries, hex wrenches for laser adjustments, a cleaning cloth, and several cleaning swabs.

This extra-wide **#70 Mag Guide By Smith & Alexander (849-011-001WB, $86)** is a drop-in one-piece mag well and mainspring housing that allows for faster, surer reloads—and you don't have to alter your pistol frame.

The Mag Guide makes the magazine-well opening 100 percent bigger and increases the pistol's grip length by ¼ inch. The larger opening makes for easier magazine insertion and faster, "can't-miss" mag changes. The extra mainspring length provides additional leverage and greater recoil control.

Brownells stocks both blued and stainless-steel Mag Guides with flat and arched housings. They fit 1911-style Government and Commander lengths and Para-Ordnance P-14s and P-16s. The Para-Ordnance models require minor modification of frames, which can be done with hand tools. Installation instructions are included in the kit.

If you're in a tight spot and can't grip your Glock's slide to operate it manually, the **#71 Tactical Supply Depot's Slide Racker (100-005-827, $35)** can be a lifesaver. The Glock Slide Racker is a replacement slide plate with an aluminum extension.

If you're in an awkward position and need to clear a jam or reload, but you can't grasp the slide to retract it, the Glock Slide Racker enables you to pull the slide backward with a fast pull of your fingers.

Depending on your tastes, you can choose from Smith & Alexander's smooth, grooved, or checkered mainspring-housing textures. The checkered models feature extra-defined 20-lines-per-inch checkering, and the grooved models present full-length vertical grooves on the mainspring housings.

The machined-aluminum Slide Racker bar is mounted perpendicular to the bore with two screws. It can be flipped for right- or left-handed operation. It's available in plain black or with an American flag logo, and it fits all Glock pistol models.

CHAPTER 5

RIFLE GADGETS

Rifle gadgets add utility, comfort, or upgraded function in various ways, and they can be inexpensive or very expensive, depending on what you're trying to accomplish.

The #72 **Ruger 10/22 50-Round Magazine from Black Dog Machine (100-005-585WB, $70)** lets you shoot long strings of .22 LR for plenty of plinking fun. The injection-molded polycarbonate drum simply snaps into the mag well like the Ruger's standard factory magazine. You don't have to modify your rifle to use the Black Dog drum.

The drum magazine's tough body and follower are self-lubricating, so they work with the constant-force spring to deliver smooth, uniform feeding. Because you're having so much fun, you may lose track of the rounds you've fired. No problem—you can see into the smoke-tinted translucent drum body to see how many rounds you have left.

Steel hex screws anchored into brass bushings securely hold the 50-Round Magazine together to ensure exceptional strength and rigidity. The screws come out easily for disassembly and cleaning.

This super-capacity magazine lets you shoot your 10/22 more and reload it less frequently.

The **#73 Ultimak AK-47 Multi-Rail Forend (100-002-178WB, $225)** allows the AK-47 owner to easily install Picatinny-rail-compatible accessories on the Kalashnikov rifle.

The hard-anodized-aluminum rail forend has MIL-STD 1913 Picatinny rails at three, six, and nine o'clock for mounting lights, lasers, and other accessories. It fits over the outside of the factory forend cap on stamped, standard-length receivers, including Chinese-manufactured AK-47s.

An expanding rear tenon system self-squares and self-centers inside the receiver and has a dual, floating steel clamp system that locks the forend to the barrel, without applying force to the barrel that can impair accuracy. Also, the forend leaves room for a bayonet on gas-block-mounted lugs.

Along with the forend, you may also want to consider the one-piece Ultimak AK-47 Scout Mounts, which are made of hard-anodized aluminum and put a single MIL-STD 1913 Picatinny top rail on the AK. Style 1 (100-000-497WB, $95) is for AK-type rifles that have original gas tubes without side gas-port holes (but does not fit the Yugo M-70 AK-47). Style 2 (100-000-

The forend has MIL-STD 1913 Picatinny rails at three, six, and nine o'clock.

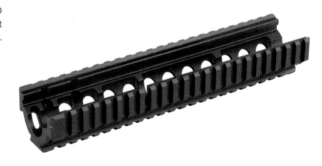

The one-piece Ultimak AK-47 Scout Mounts put a single MIL-STD 1913 Picatinny top rail on the AK. Style 1 is for AK-type rifles that have original gas tubes without side gas-port holes. Style 2 fits AK-type rifles that have original gas tubes with side gas-port holes.

The stock is designed for the heavier-contour barrels, such as in Remington's SPS, Police, and LTR models. It will work with a Sporter barrel, but will not fit as well.

177WB, $95) fits AK-type rifles that have original gas tubes with side gas-port holes. The Weaver-style base sits below the line of sight, so there's no need to remove the mount to use the factory iron sights. Also, the iron sights can be viewed directly through the red dot and reflex scopes. The forend and top mounts are sold separately, and both come with mounting tools and instructions. No gunsmithing is needed to install any of the items.

The **#74 Remington 700 AICS Stock by Accuracy International (100-005-929WB, $890)** fully assembled tactical-stock chassis converts a Remington Model 700 barreled action into a versatile long-range rifle, with no specialized gunsmithing or stock bedding needed. Simply drop a Model 700 barreled action into the Accuracy International Chassis System, or AICS, and secure the action with two bolts. The self-aligning, self-bedding aluminum "V" block chassis allows the barrel to float for superior accuracy.

The chassis is molded into a fiberglass-reinforced polymer stock that won't flex or warp, regardless of changes in temperature or humidity. The thumbhole stock has an adjustable cheekpiece and a rubber buttpad adjustable for length of pull.

The Stage 1.5 model has a conventional, fixed buttstock. The Stage 2 model has a left-folding buttstock that collapses at the thumbhole for compact storage. Both Stage 1.5 and Stage 2 stock styles come in short-action and long-action versions for the 308 Winchester and 300 Winchester Magnum, respectively. Each chassis comes with one detachable 5-round magazine.

Bolt-on spacers between the pad and the stock let you customize the length of pull. The cheekpiece adjusts vertically and horizontally for precise eye alignment with scopes and night-vision devices, and it doesn't interfere with removal of the bolt. Front and rear loops on both sides of stock accept HK-style clip-on sling swivels, while the underside of the forend includes integral attachment points for Accuracy International and Harris bipods.

Reloaders need to experiment, and sooner or later we all wind up with partially used boxes of leftover bullets, which will never be opened again. **#75 Bullet-Proof Bullet Samples (749-013-304WB, $11)** 12-piece sample packs let you test out new bullets without having to buy a box of 50 or 100 to find out what shoots well.

The idea of sample packs of bullets is not new. What is new is that Bullet Proof conveniently packages a variety of brands, calibers, weights, and styles over a range of bullet types and weights.

For instance, if you're working up a new .308 Winchester load, you might want to try these three 30-caliber Bullet Proof packages with Nosler 165-grain Accubond bullets, Barnes 168-grain Tipped TSX Boattails, and Berger 210-grain Match Hunting VLDs.

Bullet Proof Bullet Samples.

Some of the more popular packs include the .22 Caliber (.223-.224) 50-grain boattail (749-013-298WB, $6.50) and 55-grain boattail (749-013-299WB, $6.50), 264/6.5mm (.264) 120-grain (749-013-301WB, $8), and .30-caliber (.308) 150-grain E-tip, (749-013-302WB, $14.50). Other caliber selections include 20 (.204), 25 (.251), 270/6.8 mm (.277), and 338 (.338).

The **#76 AK Extended Safety by Power Custom (713-000-147WB, $60)** offers two important safety benefits for the Kalashnikov shooter. The safety's extended lower pad makes it easier to manipulate using the firing hand, so the operator can maintain eyes-up, on-the-shoulder, positive control of the rifle. Also, the hold-open notch allows the AK bolt to be locked to the rear. With the action held open, the rifle can be visually verified as safe, or the user can release the safety to quickly charge the rifle. Precision stamped from 1mm 1050 steel, these one-piece units are heat treated to 50C Rockwell hardness and are 100 percent US-made.

Gunsmith "DH" in Summerville, SC, wrote about the AK Extended Safety, "I've been using these on my Saiga conversions with no issues. I've also installed them on the Romanian and Chinese variants with good results. They're much smoother than the factory safety, and the finger lever and bolt hold open is a very nice feature. If they get too loose, simply bend them by hand to add more pressure against the receiver."

I recently tested a Century International Arms N-PAP M70 7.62x39mm. The arrow points to the cutout in the safety lever that keeps the bolt open. That's a great feature for range safety that the AK Extended Safety adds to regular Kalashnikovs.

The problem with most toolkits is that they're back in the car or at home when your AK needs work in the field or at the range. Not so with **#77 Hogue's AK-47/74 Field Survivor Pistol Grip Tool Combo (408-000-107WB, $110)**. This versatile multi-tool is like an armorer's kit that fits in the palm of your hand and stores in the pistol grip of your rifle, so you'll always have it when you need it.

The rubber "overmolded" Hogue Monogrip AK-47/74 pistol grip replaces the small, stubby original wood grip and provides a more comfortable grasp with palm swells, finger grooves, and a non-slip, knobby texture that reduces shock and improves control.

When folded, the tool slides easily into the Hogue grip, available separately or in a Combo Kit with the tool. To open, twist the base of the tool to activate the compression lock system that anchors it securely in the grip. There's no movement or rattling.

Inside is an array of tools for performing emergency repairs to get your AK back in action fast. There's a flat-blade screwdriver, broken shell extractor, pin punch, front sight adjustment tool, and a refillable stainless steel tube that holds just enough oil for one field lube. Use the wire brush for general cleaning, or remove it and attach it to the pull cable for bore cleaning, using the Survivor Tool base as a T-handle.

The grip is constructed of hardened, corrosion-resistant stainless-steel components.

The storage mechanism is encased in a tough shell of nearly indestructible reinforced polymer to ensure years of reliable service. And this bonus: the grip counts as a US-made part in compliance with 922(r) part-source requirements.

CHAPTER 6

SHOTGUN GADGETS

Scatterguns generally don't receive the same attention from aftermarket suppliers (excluding choke tubes) that rifles and pistols get. But there are some gadgets and packages that improve shotgun function. Many shooters love the Remington 870 pump shotgun in the field, and I have owned many 870s that I used for doves, ducks, and bucks. The gun has a basic appeal as a game-getter. I have also owned one self-defense version, a

Here's the refitted 870 with the Blackhawk Knoxx SpecOps Adjustable Recoil-Reducing Stock and Wilson Combat two-shot magazine extender in place.

The adjustable buttstock was much more comfortable than the original fixed stock shown, which led to a sizable upgrade overall.

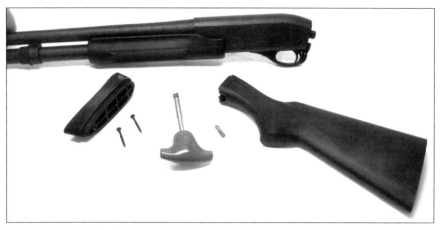

Here are the basic components of the basic 870. At left are the original butt pad and its two retaining screws. Center is the ratchet-handle driver and a bit. At right is the original stock.

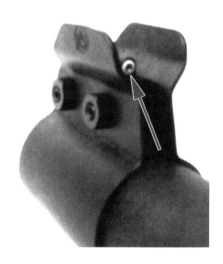

The original 870 front sight sat on a big stanchion, but the bead was unprotected. The new XS sight has a tritium capsule that glows in low-light conditions (arrow). Protective ears are part of the barrel-band mount.

using the supplied long Allen wrench, I screwed the adjustable Knoxx stock onto the gun in less than three minutes. Next, I installed the replacement forend supplied with this kit. Putting the forend on took about ten minutes with the Remington Forend Wrench, which makes getting to and removing the action nut on the 870 simple. Then I screwed on the Wilson Combat machined-steel two-shot magazine extender.

I had access to an identical 870 sans modifications, so I could compare the before-and-after guns shot to shot. Firing a range of shells from light-load 2¾-inch bird loads to 3-inch steel magnums, I immediately liked the Knoxx buttstock. It uses a spring-loaded recoil-absorption system to reduce

The full XS sight set has a Ghost Ring rear and a front tritium post. The view behind the sight is clear and much better than just a bead front sight. The XS sight is protected on the sides by substantial metal tabs. The rear aperture frames up the protective tabs in front.

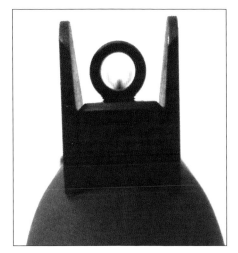

Remington Model 870 Express Magnum Synthetic 12 gauge, which I bought for $325 six years ago. The 870EMS is a capable home-defense scattergun by any measure.

But since I've become an AR owner, I love the flexibility of a six-position collapsible stock, so I began looking around for 870 replacement buttstocks. I came across the **#78 Brownells Reming-ton 870 Tactical Conversion Deluxe Kit (080-000-568WB, $290)**. It included a Blackhawk Knoxx SpecOps Adjustable Recoil-Reducing Stock and Replacement Forend, a Wilson Combat machined-steel two-shot magazine extender, which comes with a magazine spring and high-visibility chartreuse nylon follower. Also included was an XS Sight Systems Shotgun Tactical Ghost Ring Sight Set (006-000-108WB, $150). To make the job go faster, I also added a Remington Forend Wrench (080-870-202, $51).

Installing the XS Ghost Ring sight required drilling and tapping my 870's receiver, which I had done at a local gunsmith shop. Many shotguns are already drilled and tapped, and in that case, the XS sights are drop-in installs. Installing the new Knoxx buttstock was easy.

Using a ratchet-handle driver with replaceable tips, I removed the Phillips-head screws holding on the existing butt pad, and then switched bits and took out the buttstock screw. I pulled the solid buttstock off. Then, felt recoil and muzzle rise. The soft, thick rubber recoil pad was ⅝ inch thick, and it noticeably cushioned the blows of the magnums.

Of course, being able to adjust the LOP to exactly what I wanted made a big difference in fit. Also, the ergonomic plastic pistol grip with finger grooves improved control for fast follow-up shots. The ribbed replacement forend provided a good gripping surface.

The XS sights are a big upgrade over the basic 870's bead. If you intend to shoot slugs and want to hit what you're aiming at, I consider them to be vital additions.

The Phoenix Technology's KickLite Tactical Stock kits turn pump shotguns into tactical or self-defense guns. The six-position AR-style buttstock adjusts for lengths of pull from 11 ½ to 15 inches.

On my gun, I probably didn't need the Wilson mag extension to add capacity, but getting a front sling attachment was handy. If you're upgrading a shorter 870 tube, that extension increases capacity up to three shells, depending on the exact model.

#79 Phoenix Technology's KickLite Tactical Stock (100-005-357WB, $110) kits turn ordinary pump shotguns into easy-to-control tactical or self-defense guns. The six-position AR-style buttstock adjusts for lengths of pull from 11 ½ to 15 inches. The front end of the stock fits onto the rear of the shotgun action with a supplied Allen-head screw. It only takes about five minutes to swap your bird gun's fixed stock with the Phoenix stock.

Kits are available for the Remington 870 12 gauge, Mossberg's 12- and 20-gauge Models 500, 590, and 835, and the Maverick 88, and Winchester's Models 1200 and 1300 12- and 20-gauge models.

Owners of this product praise the adjustable six-position AR-style buttstock's rubber butt pad and built-in spring-loaded recoil suppression system. Those features reduce shoulder battering and improve how the gun points. A swivel stud in the buttstock accepts a swivel and sling for muzzle-down carry. The Kit includes a glass-reinforced injection-molded nylon replacement buttstock, replacement forend, screw-on shot shell holder, mounting hardware, and instructions. The five-shot 12-gauge shell carrier fits on the butt easily with the supplied screws, and takes about 2 minutes to install. The tactical forend has a deeply grooved, no-slip surface that further enhanced control.

Though you can remove your pump's current forend using regular tools, the Brownells Forend Wrench (080-870-202, $51) makes getting to and removing the action nuts easier.

Under stress, self-defense shooters can fumble when pushing the ⅜-inch-wide plastic Mossberg tang safety forward into the Fire position. **The #80 Elite Tactical Advantage Mossberg 500/590/930/935 Tactical Safety (100-005-838WB, $25)** replaces the thin factory safety switch and puts a stronger, wider, taller, and easier-to-activate toggle on Mossberg Model 500 and 590 pump guns and Model 930 and 935 autoloaders.

If you're under stress, have wet or cold hands, or you're wearing gloves, the Elite replacement safety presents an oversized, deeply ridged surface

The Elite Safety can be installed in two directions. The "wings up" position shows a steeper rearward face. It fits better on guns with traditional stocks, and shooters with large hands may prefer this orientation. If you have a pistol-grip stock or have small hands, you may prefer the "wings down" installation, which presents a larger, more sloping rear face.

that's easy to feel, find, and activate. The machined aluminum ridges on top of the Tactical Safety ensure you'll get the solid contact needed to operate the safety, even if your whole thumb isn't on the switch. Also, the large contact surface lets you operate the safety while keeping your trigger finger in the ready position alongside the receiver. The Elite Tactical Safety is just under an inch in length and width, and it's $5/16$ inch tall in the center. The safety, a steel wear plate, and an Allen-head screw are included.

#81 Mesa Tactical's Shotgun Sureshell Carrier & 20" Rail (100-006-355WB, $210) puts a full-length rail on top of the pump gun and mounts a six-slot Sureshell shot carrier on the left side of the shotgun receiver.

The top rail is useful for military, law enforcement, or self-defense shooters who want to use carbine-style back-up iron sights or night-vision optics. The rail allows optics to be mounted well in front of the receiver.

The SureShell shot shell carrier retains ammunition reliably and withstands the rigors of daily use. The carrier features an innovative rubber friction

This is Mesa Tactical's Shotgun Sureshell Carrier & 20-inch Rail (100-006-355, $210).

That's a six-slot shot shell carrier.

The rail allows optics to be mounted well in front of the receiver. No gunsmithing is required.

retention system, and it includes die-cut rubber gaskets to protect the host shotgun's finish.

The full-length rail extends past the forend and secures to the front of the gun. The saddle mount uses aluminum brackets to wrap around the top of the shotgun receiver. Internally threaded steel pins that replace the factory trigger pins fasten the mount and shot shell carrier to the receiver. No gunsmithing is required.

The saddle mount's Picatinny rail and shot shell carrier are manufactured in the United States from high-grade Mil-Spec hard-anodized aircraft aluminum. Both are bead blasted for a rugged non-glare finish.

The **#82 Side Saddle Shell Holder by Tacstar (867-105-870WB, $36)** attaches to the side of your shotgun receiver using the existing pin and screw holes, putting four or six more shot shells quickly within your reach.

The lightweight, molded-nylon shell carrier rides on an aluminum plate that fits onto the shotgun using supplied mounting screws, pins, and instructions. No permanent alterations or gunsmithing is required.

There are six-round Side Saddle Shell Holders for 12-gauge Remington 870s, 1100s, and 1187s, Benelli Super 90s, M4s, and M6s, Winchester 1200s and 1300s, and Mossberg 500s. Four-round Side Saddle Shell Holders are available for 12-gauge Benelli Novas, Mossberg 500s, and Remington 870s, 1100s, and 1187s, as well as four-round Side Saddle Shell Holders for 20-gauge 870s, 1100s, and 1187s.

Field-grade forends that extend onto the sides of the receiver must be modified or replaced to provide adequate clearance for six-shot shell holders.

This is the #82 Side Saddle Shell Holder by Tacstar (867-105-870WB, $36).

The, molded-nylon shell carrier rides on an aluminum plate. No permanent alterations or gunsmithing is required.

There are six-round as well as four-round Side Saddle Shell Holders.

CHAPTER 7

SIGHTING GADGETS

The range of options for sights is endless—dots, scopes, lasers, BUIS, to name a few. But getting them on your guns can either be done the easy way, or the not-so-easy way. Here are a few items that make the sight-mounting task a little better.

#83 Picatinny Scope Bases by Brownells (080-000-393WB, $50) provide one-piece rock-solid bases to attach scope rings on your tactical or sporter rifle. Picatinny bases offer greater flexibility than traditional ring-and-base systems, and they add rigidity to the action for more-accurate shooting.

#83 Picatinny Scope Bases by Brownells (080-000-393WB, $50) are one-piece bases.

Picatinny bases add rigidity to the action.

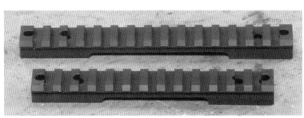

It's easy to alter spacing between the rings to accommodate different-length scope bodies. Four Torx-head screws come with all bases.

Slots in these bases are cut to true MIL-STD 1913 specs to accept both Picatinny and many Weaver-style rings, vastly increasing your scope-mounting options. You can easily alter spacing between the rings to accommodate different-length scope bodies, and adjust eye relief to fit the specific needs of each shooter.

These bases install quickly using factory-drilled scope-base holes and screws—on most guns, there's no additional drilling and tapping needed. Left-handed shooters will like these too, because the underside of the base is cut out to accommodate receivers with right- or left-hand ejection ports.

Choose between models precision machined from 4140 billet steel for superb strength and stability, or aluminum models machined from 6061 T6 billet for maximum weight reduction.

Models that will fit existing receiver-hole patterns include Howa, Weatherby, Remington, Winchester, and Savage short-action and long-action receivers. Also, there are styles for Winchester Short Magnum receivers plus military Mauser 98 rifles. Four Torx-head screws come with all bases.

The **#84 Daniel Defense One O'Clock Offset Rail (100-003-943WB, $41)** allows mounting of auxiliary optics, lights, and other accessories at convenient one o'clock or eleven o'clock positions.

One use: Clamp the lightweight low-profile rail to your AR's or M16's handguard side rail to allow easy off-axis mounting of red dot sights. This

I have found the DD Offset Rail to be a perfect mount for my Burris Fastfire on an 18-inch SPR.

The offset rail allows easy transition from scope at top center over to the red dot at one o'clock and back without changing cheek weld. It works better than having to raise the eye off the scope.

allows the operator to transition almost instantly from long-range primary optic to non-magnified CQB sight without breaking cheek weld.

Another use: Install the Offset Rail on the underside of the handguard to position a laser or weapon light close to the vertical forend grip. That makes for easy operation of controls with your support hand.

Use the Offset Rail with backup iron sights, too. The side bar and cross bolt locking system ensures secure, zero-movement attachment to the primary rail. Remove and reinstall your BUIS without losing zero. A viewing tunnel through the mount allows the operator to see around the target.

The **#85 Dueck Defense AR-15/M16 Rapid Transition Sight System (100-006-162WB, $240)** provides the competitive, LE, or military tactical

Made of hardcoat-anodized 7075 aluminum the Dueck sights install with a slot-tip screwdriver.

The Dueck front sight is 1 ⅜ inches long, 3 inches wide, and weighs 3.1 ounces.

The Dueck machined aluminum RTS backup sights mount at a 45° offset angle to enable instant transition from the primary optic simply by tilting the rifle.

The Dueck rear sight is 1 inch long, 2 ¾ inches wide, and weighs 1 ½ ounces.

shooter with the quickest transition possible from optical to offset iron sights. These offset sights greatly increase the shooter's accuracy when dealing with near and far targets, and they eliminate the need to co-witness backup sights through an optic.

The sight's designer, top 3-Gun shooter and IPSC Grand Master Barry Dueck (pronounced "deck"), realized that when shooting close targets on the move, he was more effective with standard M4/M16 iron sights than with anything else. But he needed an optical sight for longer ranges. The RTS sight design makes the iron sights and optics become independent sighting systems that are always ready. The sights can be installed on the left or right side of receiver, and they provide the same bore height and sight picture as standard USGI A2 sights. The RTS A2-style rear sight has flip-up long- and short-range apertures, and is adjustable for windage and elevation in ½-minute-of-angle clicks. The locking bar and cross-bolt attachment system clamps securely to MIL-STD 1913 Picatinny rails and sits only two-tenths of an inch above the rail, so there's no interference with the main sighting system. The front sight base won't interfere with the beam path of military IR laser/illuminators.

#86 One-Piece Flat-Top Optic Mounts from JP Enterprises (452-000-124WB, $185) allow AR owners to mount or dismount optics as a single unit for fast, precise changeovers. The aluminum mounts, precision machined to MIL-STD 1913 specs, contain integral rings tall enough to accommodate 56mm objective lenses on riflescopes. The full-length base employs five Torx-key cross bolts to securely and accurately fasten the mount to your rifle's rail. If you need to remove the optics, just unscrew the mount from the rail and

On the #86 One-Piece Flat-Top Optic Mounts from JP Enterprises, the forward offset of the front ring provides room to adjust the scope's eye-relief precisely for the shooter's needs.

lift off the scope, rings, and mount as one piece. Then, if you need to reinstall the scope, the assembly goes back on the gun with minimal change in zero.

Six Allen-head screws secure the scope into each ring for a rock-solid installation. The actual centerline heights of the rings are 1 ½ inches over the rail, ideal for AR applications. There are two versions, one for 34mm-diameter main tubes and another for 35mm tubes. On both, the edges have been radiused to knock off sharp corners, and both incorporate an integrated recoil lug.

The **#87 Tech Sights GI Type Aperture Sight Assemblies for the Ruger 10-22 Rifle (100-006-911WB, $70)** substantially upgrade the rimfire's buckhorn-and-post open sights, improving accuracy and making the semi-auto's sight picture look more like your AR's.

The rear sight base mounts solidly to the rear receiver using the 10-22's tapped scope-base holes. To install the front sight, use a brass punch to tap on the base of the front sight and drive the front sight blade out of the dovetail slot from left to right. Then slide or tap the Tech Sights' sight tower into the dovetail slot, right to left, until it is centered on the barrel. Detailed instructions are included. Once installed, the new sights offer eight more inches of sight radius and a lot of adjustability. At the muzzle, the steel front sight is an adjustable AR-15 type post with incremental detent. It's compatible with standard AR-15 or M16 posts. The rear sight bases are hardcoat-anodized black aluminum. Both rear sights comes with dual leaf apertures, and both accept AR-15 and M16 apertures should you wish to swap them. The TSR100 is windage adjustable, with each click-detent delivering about ⅝ inch of movement at 100 yards. The TSR200 allows for additional elevation adjustment at the rear sight.

The TSR200 rear sight, shown, allows for elevation adjustment. The steel front sight is an adjustable AR-15 type post.

CHAPTER 8

TRANSPORT GADGETS

Getting guns and gear from point A to point B can be done in any number of ways. Schlepping them in ill-fitting and hard-to-handle cases is one way. But there are other solutions.

The brand name Hazard 4 is derived from the familiar 1 through 4 classification of threats, in which "4" means potentially deadly. So when Hazard 4 built these **#88 Messenger Of Doom Go Bags (100-010-568WP, $141)**, the bags were meant to carry the user's last lines of defense.

The M.O.D., or Messenger Of Doom, Bags are versions of Hazard 4's versatile Ditch Bag. Inside these unassuming Cordura 1000-denier exteriors are multiple solutions for carrying weapons. In fact, a lawyer acquaintance of mine carries a Kel-Tec Sub-2000 in his Messenger Of Doom Bag, twenty-four/seven.

Internal loop-fasteners allow the user to attach a modular holster. Or, internal and external wide belts accommodate belt-slide type holsters, and

The Doom Go Bag also includes front loop fasteners for patches, a drop-down shelf work-area with document/map window, and a full organizer for pens, knives, flashlights, magazines, and other gear.

The Universal system will work with most generic hip nylon holsters, outside-the-waistband Kydex holsters such as BlackHawk!, Fobus, and SafariLand, or even inside-the-waistband holsters, provided there is a belt loop, belt clip, or slots. Paddle holsters are not recommended.

side flat-pockets can carry paddle-type holsters. And the M.O.D.'s three flat pockets hold any full-sized auto-pistol.

Roomy at 17.75 inches long, 12.6 inches tall, and 5.5 inches thick, the M.O.D. accepts up to a 17-inch MacBook Pro or 16-inch PC, a folding-stock carbine, a folding or telescopic-stock submachine gun, and a section of ballistic-armor plate, depending on your needs.

The messenger can load-out several modular containers on the Bag's front surface but keep the compartments hidden under the unassuming flap. The flap compresses bulk with oversized lock-buckle-straps, and the straps or the flap itself can be removed in a few seconds.

Quick and accessible, the **#89 Universal Vehicle Holster Mount & Adaptor by Gum Creek Customs (100-006-549WB, $35)** is ideal for carrying a handgun in a duty or personal vehicle. The mount and adaptor are not vehicle or firearm specific, and one size fits all steering columns.

Install the mount directly into the gap below the steering-wheel column and secure the mount at the bottom of the dash/kick panel. The adaptor allows installation on steering columns that don't have a gap.

Use any common type of holster with a belt loop, belt clip, or slotted belt attachment and attach it to the mount. The mount and adaptor will fit and support most common holsters and small or large handguns, due to the mount having an internal metal support bar as part of the main frame. The support bar stiffens the mount and keeps the rig from sagging and turning.

Most hunters know that it is not the weight of the rifle that makes it feel heavy in the field. Instead, you get fatigued by the constant up, down, and side-to-side shock the rifle generates while you walk or climb. **#90 Vero Vellini Air Cushion Rifle Slings (100-000-047WB, $30)** are designed to absorb that extra shock. Pioneers of the neoprene sling, Vero Vellini sets itself apart with its three-layer Air-Cushion neoprene sandwich construction that makes a sling comfortable, but not bouncy. The neoprene, combined with other flexible materials, creates a sling that will stretch slightly with every step  and absorb the shock generated by walking or hiking. The high-density rubber backing keeps the pad from slipping off your shoulder. Durable outer straps of 1-inch nylon webbing have double-stitched leather end caps for a firm grasp during length adjustments. Two steel friction buckles keep your chosen length locked in tight.

The **#91 AR-15/M16 Ultra-Compact Discreet Rifle Case made by Bulldog Cases (100-005-304WB, $28)** provides discreet concealment and maximum protection for a short-barreled AR, a rifle disassembled into upper and lower halves, or other expensive gear during transport.

The navy blue Discreet Case (photos on next page) features a durable, heavy-duty, water-resistant Tetron outer shell and 2½-inch thick foam padding that provides a snug, firm hold on the gun. A heavy-duty zipper with large aluminum pull tabs discreetly allows for an easy grasp and open with a thumb and forefinger. Protecting the gun's finish inside the case is a no-scratch lining of brushed Tricot that won't sag, billow, or deform.

Bulldog's Discreet Case measures 29 inches in length, is 3 inches deep, and stands 11 inches high.

Inside, there's a full-length padded divider that has two mag pouches double stitched into one side.

The divider keeps loose magazines from damaging your gun or from rattling around indiscreetly.

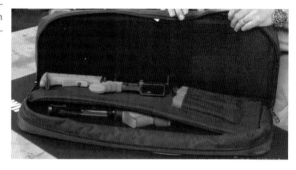

CHAPTER 9

HANDY GADGETS

No, the items in this chapter are not on most people's "must have" lists. But they are on my "nice to have" list. The next time you go to the range with your bag of 30-round magazines, be sure to take along a bag of quarters, too. Because every time you fire a round and don't retrieve your brass, you're essentially tossing 25 cents on the ground.

The **#92 AR-15/M16 Brass-Savr Brass Catcher by 3 Bucc Inc. (100-000-735WB, $60)** can put that money—your spent brass—back into your pocket. And you don't have to crawl on the ground to collect the cases. The Brass Catcher's cotton-poly bag and non-scratching polymer mount hook onto your AR or M16. When you fire a round, it ejects into the Brass Catcher. Supported by steel frame, the Brass Catcher holds 70 rounds of .223 brass. When it's full, the easy-open bottom unloads the fired cases fast.

Getting your guns and gear on and off the range is a lot easier with the **#93 Mac Sports Folding Utility Wagon (100-005-219WB, $80)**. This

There are two Brass-Savr models to fit ARs with carry handles and flattop AR-style rifles. The bag measures 4 ¼ inch wide, 3 ½ inch long, and 7 ¼ inch deep.

The #93 Mac Sports Folding Utility wagon folds conveniently by pulling up on a handle in the floor. Securing the two straps keeps it closed. There's no assembly required.

27-pound utility wagon folds flat enough to fit in a car trunk, then when unfolded, it holds up to 150 pounds of equipment.

When folded, the wagon measures 8 inches long, 20 ¼ inches wide, and 29 ½ inches high. To expand it, the shooter stands the wagon up on the rear wheels, undoes two straps, and gently pulls the wagon open—all in about five seconds. The strong steel frame and durable 600-denier nylon body, with a sturdy padded plastic floor, provide plenty of support for heavy loads. Once open, the wagon is 36 inches long, 20 inches wide, and 23 inches high, roomy enough to hold three or more guns, a bench rest, targets, cleaning supplies, ammunition, and more. A series of padded panels can be added by attaching them to hook-and-loop strips in the wagon sidewalls.

The **#94 Competitive Edge Dynamics's M2 Chronograph System (399-000-012WB, $200)** is a substantial upgrade of the highly regarded original CED Millennium Chronograph. New advanced technology enabled

Included with the CED M2 are the chronograph, sensors, cables, screen-mounting bracket, USB computer interface cable, and the new CED Data Collector Software program.

All you need to add is a 9-volt battery and tripod to mount the screen bracket on.

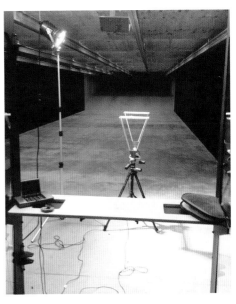

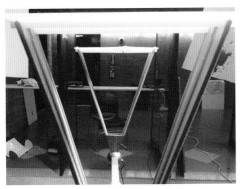

An optional Infrared Screen Set permits chronograph use in all light conditions, even total darkness, indoors or out. An AC adapter powers the sensors. Or you can just add an external light source as shown here to run the unit indoors.

CED to double the operating speed of the M2 chronograph while expanding the operation range from 50 fps to 7,000 fps. An expanded digital chip design allows the M2 to read velocities at much lower light levels. On clear days, this means the ability to chronograph from early morning till almost sunset.

The new M2's memory storage has also been vastly expanded. The original Millennium unit stored 220 velocities. With the M2, a stored string size can range from a single velocity up to 500 velocities, and M2 stores data for up to 500 different strings.

There's a host of other new features as well, including a keypad with a calculator-style layout, a built-in calculator, one-touch calculation of the average of the three highest velocities in a string—ideal for calculating Power Factor at IPSC and IDPA matches, and much more. The optional Cordura case stores all the chronograph parts, screens, screen bracket and cables. The case has loops on the outside to attach to your tripod.

The **#95 CED7000 Shot-Activated Timer by Competitive Edge Dynamics (399-000-008WB, $130)** is a full-featured timer that's so compact you'll forget you're wearing it. Now you can hone your shooting times with a unit that's roughly the size of a cell phone and just as easy to operate.

Despite its small size, the CED7000 is packed with features for shooters who want to go faster. A custom par setting allows you train against single or multiple time settings. There's also a Multi-Par mode that initiates multiple Par settings from one timer activation.

Variable delay intervals can be set to 0.01 of a second, and there's a 999.99-second time-recording capacity. A combined Comstock function calculates scores simply and easily. There's a Countdown Mode, and the Timer has unlimited shot record and review.

The unit's digital sensitivity shot detector has an adjustable software filter to ensure accurate, fair results. The easy-to-read illuminated LCD screen displays split- and first-time shots on each shot fired,

For match use, the CED7000 has built-in auxiliary jack signals an external loud horn, visual start system, or target turning mechanisms. Plus, it can be upgraded for wireless connection to a CED BigBoard

The 7000 runs on a built-in rechargeable battery, and it comes with a universal plug-in charger. Wrist and neck lanyards are included, and a black high-impact-plastic case makes storage and transport a snap.

or CED Time Keeper for displaying results up to 50 yards away from the timer.

If you want to be comfortable when you're shooting at the bench or when reloading, the **#96 Shooting Stool by Sinclair International (749-007-602WS, $105)** offers a padded, weather-resistant seat, stands rock solid, and accommodates different bench heights.

The padded 14-inch seat is extremely comfortable. Perhaps as important, the seat height can be adjusted inside an 8-inch range, putting your body at the right height to shoot at ranges across the country or work at your bench for extended periods. Pull this lever and the stool's pneumatic stem-height adjustment can be locked in from a collapsed height of about 17 inches to an extended height around 25 inches.

The five legs provide a very stable platform. And the three major parts—seat, stem, and base—come apart easily so they'll lay flat while in transit.

#97 GunVault MicroVault and Mini-Vault Pistol Safes (100-006-689WB, $100) are notebook-style units that allow you to securely transport your handgun or valuables inside a briefcase or day pack, yet you can still you can get inside the safes quickly with GunVault's No-Eyes keypad technology.

Each safe is constructed of heavy-gauge steel, and its precise fittings are next to impossible to pry open with hand tools. However, in seconds, the owner can operate the safe's finger-groove keypads to release a high-strength lock. Then, a spring-activated vault door pops open, giving the owner easy access to the gun inside.

Model GV1000-CSTD, the MiniVault's 16-gauge case, is just over 12 inches in length and about 8 inches wide. Closed, it's about 5 inches tall and weighs 9 pounds empty. It runs on eight AA batteries.

Model MV500-STD, the MicroVault's exterior is 11 inches long and 8 ½ inches wide. Closed, it's 2 ¼ inches thick and weighs 5 pounds empty. The interior, fitted with soft foam, offers 10 ¾ inches of storage length and 6 ½ inches of width, with 2 inches of depth.

#98 Omega Safety Systems Chamber Locks (100-006-979WB, $20) are internal gunlocks that help prevent unauthorized gun use and accidental

A built-in computer in the the Mini Vault blocks access after repeated invalid entries, and if you're traveling, a 4-foot security cable ties the safes down when you're away.

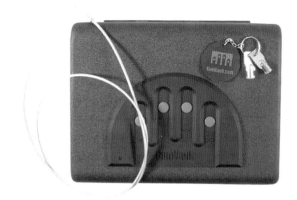

There are audible and LED low-battery warnings to ensure the Mini Vault safes stay functional, and they mount almost anywhere.

Because an Omega lock is the same size as empty brass for a specific gun, the lock fits inside a gun's chamber.

This internal design makes Omega locks caliber specific—not gun specific—and are more secure than external gunlocks.

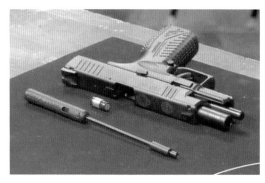

In revolvers, the lock goes through the cylinder, into the barrel, and locks the cylinder, trigger, and hammer, freezing the entire gun.

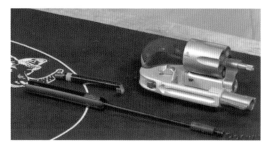

discharge while maintaining a fast emergency release that can have your gun ready to fire in less than five seconds.

Here is how they work. The owner inserts a caliber-specific Omega lock into a gun's chamber. He then uses a provided key to engage the lock in the chamber. Turning the key causes a soft aluminum ring to expand inside the chamber. For automatic pistols, the lock engages the extractor, locks the slide onto the frame, and renders the gun inoperable. In revolvers, the lock goes through the cylinder, into the barrel, and locks the cylinder, trigger, and hammer, freezing the entire gun.

Because Omega gunlocks are softer than ammunition brass, they cannot damage the gun in any way. Also, they are invisible and do not distract from the workmanship of the gun.

A range of Omega locks are available for the most common centerfire handgun chambers, including 9mm Parabellum, .380 ACP, .40 S&W, .45 ACP, .38 Special, and .357 Magnum.

Edgewood Leather's premium bags and shooting accessories are innovative, made of the best materials available, and will hold up under constant competitive use. Edgewood Leather products are made by benchrest shooter Jack Snyder, who also owns one of the best-known bridleworks in the country. Edgewood craftsmen know how to select and fashion leather into functional, durable, and beautiful shooting accessories.

For instance, the **#99 Edgewood Minigator Rear Bag (749-007-873WB, $150)** has a large 6 ½- by 10-inch footprint, with taller and longer ears than many other bags. This bag is popular with free-recoil shooters because of its supreme tracking qualities. For the forend, Edgewood Front Benchrest Bags (749-006-366WB, $64) are constructed much like the Minigator Rear Bags. The Front Bags have reinforced-leather sides and heavy-duty nylon tops, and the inside corners feature sewn-in nylon inserts to prevent the material from rolling under the forend.

There are four styles of Edgewood Front Bags available. The Standard Front Bag style has half-inch leather flaps extending along the bottom edges, which can be pinned under your rest-top retaining bars. Or the flaps

The Edgewood Minigator Rear Bag weighs about 13 to 16 pounds when filled with heavy sand, making it a rock-solid buttstock anchor for bench shooting. I recommend filling the Minigator with Sinclair's Heavy Bag Sand (749-003-070WS, $20). It's sold in 15-pound boxes, which is enough to fill the Minigator Rear Bag with a little left over. Below left is a front bag that fits on your front rest. Below is the Elbow Pad.

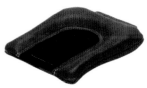

may be punched, notched, or cut away to custom-fit your rest. There's also a Standard Front Bag style with a reinforced top. It's extra thick on top to hold your desired forend's shape. Then there's the Farley Front Bag style, which is narrower than the Standard Front Bag front to back. It's made specifically to fit the Farley Co-Axial and Co-Axial II rests. Edgewood also makes a Farley Front Bag with a reinforced top. These styles all come in two widths: 2 ¼-inch wide openings fit hunter stocks, and the bags with 3-inch openings fit benchrest stocks.

Along with those front bags, I also recommend the Edgewood Elbow Pad (749-006-346WB, $64), a U-shape formed-leather piece with a non-skid bottom and stitched nylon insert. It helps you maintain a consistent index to the gun, which is part of producing small groups. And, naturally, these pre-filled pads keep the concrete bench from scraping your elbow.

The **#100 Laser Training Target by Laserlyte (100-009-731WB, $150)** offers shooters the ability to practice shooting skills inexpensively at almost any location. For use with LaserLyte's line of **#101 Laser Trainers (100-006-951WB, $80)** the Trainer Target is ideal for shooters to learn or teach shooting skills, such as unsighted fire, accuracy, grouping, and trigger control.

To use the Laser Trainer Target, simply aim at the target and dry-fire an unloaded weapon with any LaserLyte Laser Trainer device. To display impact, fire the laser at the red display circle on the face of the Laser Trainer Target. When finished, dry-fire the laser at the red reset circle to start with a fresh target.

The #100 Laser Training Target by Laserlyte 100-009-731WB is used in tandem with Laser Trainers 100-006-951WB, which emit a beam when struck by the firing pin.

The LaserLyte Laser Trainer Target operates with three AA batteries, good for about 6,000 shots, and can register shots up to 50 yards away. The Laser Trainer Target contains 62 laser-activated LED lights and operates without use of a computer, television or projector.

With a Laser Trainer laser inserted into an empty chamber and the unloaded gun made ready to fire, aim at the target and dry-fire the unloaded weapon.

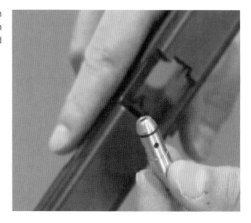

The hit is displayed as a lighter area on the target.

CHAPTER 10

HONORABLE MENTIONS

T
he Merriam-Webster definition of *lagniappe* is "a small gift given a customer by a merchant at the time of a purchase; broadly, something given or obtained gratuitously or by way of good measure." So here's a bit of *lagniappe*: there are some other items I considered for this book, but which didn't make the cut for the 101 Gadgets List. Nonetheless, they are interesting, and I touch on them briefly below.

Brownells stopped carrying the **AR-15/M16 AR57 Upper Receiver by 57 Center** during the production of this book, but it's still available directly from the manufacturer. This Upper Receiver by 57 Center converts your AR-15 to fire soft-shooting 5.7x28mm ammunition

The receiver uses blowback operation with a free-sliding bolt that's the only moving part, which means there's no gas system to foul or clog with

AR-15/M16 AR57 Upper Receiver by 57 Center, $745.

carbon. The 50-round magazines run horizontally along the top of the action, and fired cases are ejected downward through the empty magwell.

The AR57 PDW 5.7X28mm Upper comes with a 17.75-inch-long, 2.77-inch-tall monolithic receiver/handguard rail machined from aluminum that offers nearly 3 feet of Picatinny rail space for mounting optics and other accessories. The rear rail contains the mag retention system. The unit itself measures 24.9 inches in O.A.L. and weighs 4.6 lbs. The receiver/handguard is made of 7075 T6 aluminum, hardcoat anodized, in matte-black finish. The barrel is 4140 chrome-moly steel with a matte-black Parkerized finish and has a 1:8.5-inch twist and ½x28 threads on the front to accept the standard A2 flash suppressor. The magazines are translucent, smoke-colored molded polymer sticks.

There are many similarities between the AR57 PDW and FN's PS90 and P90 bullpup carbines, besides being chambered for 5.7x28mm ammunition. The FN guns use 10- or 30-round magazines that run horizontally along the top of the action, and fired cases are ejected downward. In the AR57 upper, it sits on top of an AR-15 lower, and empties are ejected down through the empty magwell. The AR57 I tested came with a single 50-round FN-style polymer magazine. Some AR57 users take an AR-15 magazine and remove the guts, then insert the blank mag in the gun to catch expelled 5.7 brass. Elsewhere, the AR57 has a 16.04-inch-long ER Shaw barrel with integral muzzle brake. The action is blowback operation and fires from a closed bolt. The free-sliding bolt is the only moving part, which means there's no gas system to keep clean.

At the range, I enjoyed shooting the AR57/CMMG. One of the advantages of the magazine's top and forward-mounted location on the AR57 upper receiver is better bench and prone shooting. Without a long magazine protruding from the bottom of a regular AR, it's possible to get a lower slung-in firing position, and mag changes can be made by rolling slightly to the left (right-handed shooter) without raising up to clear a long under-gun magazine. Also, I liked that the shooter's support hand and arm can be put directly under the rifle in offhand, kneeling, and prone positions without banging into a long magazine.

Operationally, loading the 50-round magazines was interesting and time consuming. There's a circular table on one end of the magazine, and as rounds are pushed down into a cartridge slot, the table rotates 90 degrees clockwise to locate the round sideways in the magazine. To insert the magazine into the upper, the shooter pushes the magazine into the front latch first, then snaps the circular end down on top of the action. Then, he pulls the charging handle on the right of the unit to chamber a round. During my shooting, I had one failure to fire when the bolt didn't fully close. I worked the charging handle backward then released it forward, and the round chambered then fired when I pulled the trigger.

Arredondo's AR-15 M16 Monopod 60 (069-000-037WB, $20) slips onto the bottom of Surefire 60-round magazines, allowing the magazine to be used as a monopod without damaging the floor plate. The Monopod's 30 percent glass-filled-nylon construction is tough, so it protects the Surefire's floor plate from rocks or concrete during prone shooting or when the operator needs to steady the rifle on any surface.

The Arredondo AR-15 M16 Monopod 60 also protects a fully loaded Surefire from damage if the magazine is dropped. Installation does not require removing the existing floor plate.

Bob Hahin designed the **Original AR-15 Bob Sled Single-Round Loading Device (749-005-593WS, $44)** as a single-round loading device for AR-15 and similar pattern rifles used in competition, at the bench, or while out varmint shooting. The Bob Sled is a magazine that holds no rounds, allowing the shooter to load and fire a single cartridge—especially valuable for long rounds that will not function out of a standard magazine. CNC machined from black Delrin, the Long Bob Sled operates and feels like a standard 20-round magazine. The Short Bob Sled mimics the handling characteristics of a 10-round AR magazine.

To use, insert the Bob Sled in the rifle instead of a magazine. When the bolt is opened, the built-in plunger trips the bolt catch and holds the bolt open. Then place a single round in the ejection port, where it rests in the

Original Bob Sleds are available in a short length for match-rifle shooters and a long length for CMP/NRA Service rifles shooters. It's approved for competition use by the NRA and CMP. If you shoot High Power rifles across the course with an AR rifle, the Bob Sled is a great choice for the standing and prone slow-fire positions.

Sled's loading channel, perfectly aligned with the chamber. Press the bolt-release button, and the rifle chambers the single round. When that round is fired, the action cycles normally and the Sled's plunger trips the bolt-catch lever to hold the bolt open.

To charge your AR-style carbine, current CQB techniques have the operator racking the charging handle to the rear using the support-side-hand only. Extended tactical latches have made this movement much more efficient, but they put a lot of stress on a tiny $\frac{1}{16}$-inch roll pin in the latch. **Bravo Company's AR-15/M16 BCM Gunfighter Charging Handle (100-005-369, $48)** features internal redesigns to direct force off the roll pin and into the body of the charging handle during support-hand-only manipulations.

This new design has a built-in backstop engineered into the extended latch and into the charging handle. As the latch is opened, its travel is limited by the backstop, taking stress off the roll pin. Because the tiny roll pin is no longer the weak point, the Gunfighter handle is a much stronger system. The tactical latch will stay intact

There are three Gunfighter handles, a Medium-length extended latch and a Large latch. The Large latch is ¼ inch longer for an even bigger grasping surface on the handle. Both latches are constructed from 7075 T6 aluminum and are Mil-Spec Type III hardcoat anodized. The Ambi Charging Handle features a latch on both the left- and right-hand sides.

even under repeated manipulation. And because force stays inside the body of the handle, the handle moves directly to the rear, making for smoother operation.

The **Brownells Barrel Extension Torque Tool for AR-15s and M16s (080-000-637WB, $38)** helps the shooter apply straight-line torque for fast, easy installation of the barrel nut without scratching the exterior of the upper receiver. The tool ensures the right amount of torque is evenly applied, while maintaining proper alignment of the barrel, upper receiver, and gas-tube ports. Use it with any barrel-nut wrench or free-float tube wrench and a torque wrench with a half-inch square drive, available separately. Simply clamp the barrel-nut wrench handle firmly in a bench vise, insert the barrel into the upper receiver, and finger-tighten the barrel nut. Then, slide the barrel through the wrench, and insert the Torque Tool into the back of the receiver until the teeth lock into the locking lugs in the receiver extension. Use the half-inch drive to apply torque through the tool to tighten the barrel nut.

The Torque Tool is precision machined from heavy-duty steel barstock for years of reliable service. It's 9 inches long and has a 1-inch diameter. Made in the United States, it fits barrel extensions of the AR-15, M16, M4, and clones chambered in .223 Remington or 5.56mm NATO only.

Brownells AR-15/M16 Buttstock Mounting Kits (080-000-620WB, $200) contain the original factory parts needed to securely mount the buttstock of your choice using original factory parts from the manufacturer of your receiver. Having a complete parts kit for the job eliminates the hassle of tracking down every part and accidentally getting incorrect ones for your stock. The kit includes everything you need to finish your build, so you won't be held up waiting for that one part you forgot to order.

The A1 Rifle kit is for mounting any fixed buttstock based on the military M16A1 stock. The kit includes a receiver extension tube, recoil buffer, buffer spring, and buttstock screw.

Select the buttstock you want, available separately, then purchase the Buttstock Mounting Kit for that type of stock. Each kit contains original factory parts. Parts from one manufacturer will fit another manufacturer's receiver, but may require minor fitting.

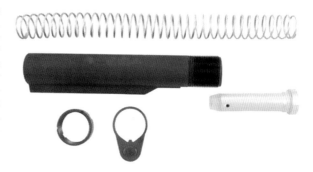

The A2 Rifle kit is for mounting any fixed buttstock based on the military M16A2 stock. This kit includes a receiver extension tube, recoil buffer, buffer spring, buttstock spacer, and buttstock screw. The A1 and A2 Rifle receiver extension measures 10 ⅛ inches in overall length.

The Mil-Spec Carbine kit is for adjustable-length carbine buttstocks that require an M4-type buffer tube with a 1.14-inch outer diameter. The Mil-Spec kit includes a receiver extension tube, carbine recoil buffer, buffer spring, receiver plate, and lock nut. The Mil-Spec Carbine receiver extension is 7 ¼ inches long overall. There are six locking positions for the buttstock, unless otherwise indicated.

The Commercial Carbine kit is set up for adjustable-length carbine buttstock that require what's known as a commercial buffer tube with a 1.17-inch outer diameter. Otherwise, it has the same components as the Mil-Spec kit. The receiver extension length is 7 ¾ inches for this kit. The extension supports six locking positions.

There are also brand-specific kits. The Colt kits, for instance, include parts from the original manufacturer of the M16 battle rifle. Colt kits for the A1 Rifle, A2 Rifle, and Mil-Spec Carbine kits are available. FYI, the Carbine kit contains the four-position Mil-Spec receiver extension used on the Colt M4 and Law Enforcement carbines. The DPMS kit holds factory parts used in the popular Panther rifle series. DPMS-specific kits come in three versions for A2 Rifle, Mil-Spec, and Commercial Carbine. Kits for High Standard rifles use original parts found in the HSA-15 series of rifles and carbines. Commercial Carbine and fixed A2 Rifle kits are available in the HS line.

I've found that most scope rings aren't mounted in true alignment. And rings that aren't aligned can stress your scope's main tube, causing accuracy deficiencies. Fortunately, scope rings can be checked for precise alignment—

The kit contains the new Sinclair International Scope Ring Alignment Tool and Scope Ring Lapping Tools. They come fitted into a Scope Installation Storage Case. Inside the protective case you'll find one set of Sinclair Scope Alignment Tools, 1-inch and 30mm Scope Ring Lapping Tools, one Lapping Tool Handle, and one container of our lapping compound. If you already own the Alignment Tools or Lapping Tools, the storage case is also available separately.

and corrected—with **Sinclair's International Scope Ring Lapping Tool Combo Kit (749-011-661, $170).**

The Scope Ring Alignment Tool will enable any shooter to properly align and install any style of 30mm and 1-inch scope rings from any manufacturer. This Alignment Tool goes beyond the traditional pointed-rod-style tools, in that the alignment rods are adjustable within the two tool bodies after the bodies are mounted in the scope rings. There's no more loosening the rings several times to adjust the rod-point lengths. The rods are held in the tool bodies by precision-machined collets that fit 1-inch and 30mm rings.

With the tool bodies and alignment rods in place, check the position of the rods midway between the sleeves. They should be barely touching, and if they're coaxially aligned, the two rod ends should meet. If the Alignment Tool identifies that the rings are out of line, then you can correct the problem in a couple of ways.

Use the scope-alignment rods to manipulate the scope rings. Apply a reasonable force on the ring to bring the alignment pointers together. This can be performed on both rings in moderation. But don't attempt too much correction this way. Another option when there's minimal misalignment is to rotate the rings 180°, which may produce better alignment. A better choice is using the kit's Lapping Tools, which remove metal from the inside of the scope rings. This procedure puts the bearing surface of each ring in alignment with the other.

Sinclair Scope Ring Lapping Tools are made from ground accuracy stock stainless steel that has a tolerance of plus or minus 0.0005 of an inch. The Lapping Tool bars are 10 inches long, which give you plenty of stroke length to quickly lap the rings. To use the lapping kit, put the handle on the lapping bar, then place the bar in the rings and lightly tighten them. You should still be able to move the bar back and forth with a little effort. Then apply the lapping compound to the bar, and vigorously move the bar back and forth in the rings.

The fine-grit compound removes small amounts of metal from the rings. Check frequently to see how the bearing surfaces look. Once the compound has removed metal evenly from the interior surfaces of the rings, they'll be in alignment and will offer the most bearing surface on the scope tube.

Hawkeye Precision Borescopes (749-008-478WB, $970) are valuable tools to help target shooters, benchrest shooters, varmint hunters, gunsmiths, and everyday hunters get the most out of their rifle barrels. You'll be amazed at the view this easy-to-use device delivers. The Hawkeye Borescope gives you a magnified view inside a rifle barrel. You know precisely what's there, without guessing. Without a borescope, you can't know what's going on inside your rifle bore because you can't see into it.

Hawkeye Borescopes have been upgraded recently, with even better optics and improved mirror technology to provide a sharper, clearer picture of the rifle bore. The Shooter's Edition kit includes a 17-inch borescope with a focusing eyepiece for viewing straight down the bore, a mirror adapter for

Many shooters use Hawkeye Borescopes to check for erosion and fouling problems. Also, the borescope can show if reamer marks been lapped out, if major blemishes are visible, and if the chamber throat was cut concentrically.

For maintenance, the bore-scope shows how smooth the chamber and throat are, if a cleaner works, and how much more scrubbing might be necessary. Also, use the borescope to determine how fouled the bore is and where fouling occurs. Outside the bore, the scope can also be used to examine the interior of loading dies, cartridge cases, and lug recesses.

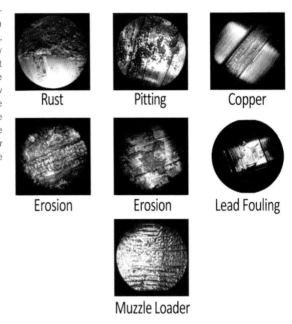

Rust   Pitting   Copper

Erosion   Erosion   Lead Fouling

Muzzle Loader

looking 90° into the sidewall of the barrel, a light source, and a hard storage case. If you already own a Hawkeye Borescope, an angled eyepiece is also available separately.

No one likes having to remove a live round stuck in a rifle chamber. A stuck round presents a difficult and potentially dangerous situation regardless of the cause, such as an oversize case, a dirty or rough chamber, or attempting to chamber the wrong ammunition. The **Brownells Stuck Case Puller (080-880-308WB, $126)** allows the Range Officer, shooter, or gunsmith to safely remove live rounds from most styles of centerfire rifles that fire a rimless cartridge.

It works best on those designs that allow access to the chamber from the rear. This would include most bolt-action and single-shot rifles. But the tool can also be used to pull rounds from the chambers of pump and auto-loading rifles whose barrels can be readily removed from the receiver. In the case of firearms that do not allow rear access to the chamber, the barrel should be unscrewed from the receiver. Then the tool is used to pull the round. This may seem drastic, but removing a live round is dangerous, so it's better to be cautious.

Be careful using the Brownells Stuck Case Puller. A firearm with a stuck live round must be treated with the same care given to any loaded

gun. Special attention must be paid to the direction the muzzle is pointed, but at the same time, the operator should not expose himself to danger at the breech end of the gun. When the powder inside a loaded case is ignited, pressure is exerted equally in all directions. The force will follow the path of least resistance, and because the case usually offers less resistance than the bullet, it may exit the gun whole or in pieces, often at great velocity.

Although it may not be necessary to remove the barreled action from the stock to use the Brownells Stuck Case Puller, we strongly urge you to do so. This will prevent damage to the stock and finish from the slide hammer portion of the Stuck Case Puller.

Next, remove the bolt from bolt-action rifles or rifles where the chamber may be accessible from the rear of the action. Verify that the body of the tool can be inserted into the receiver up to the chamber. Depending on the make and model of the rifle, it may be necessary to remove the bolt stop, ejector, and even the trigger assembly.

Select the proper collet. They are available in three case-head dimensions. The small version fits cases with a head diameter of .378 inch, such as the .221, .222, and .223. The mid-size collet fits "standard" .473-inch size cases. The large collet is used with belted magnum cases with a head diameter of .532 inch. Verify that you have the correct collet by checking it against a cartridge of the same caliber as the one you are attempting to remove.

Assemble the puller body, collet, draw rod, and knurled connector sleeve. Leave the collet open so it can surround the case head. Slide the unit into the receiver until the case head bottoms out within the collet. Use the sleeve holding pin to hold the puller body stationary with pressure exerted forward, toward the muzzle. Rotate the knurled connector sleeve or the puller body to tighten the collet. Give it a tug rearward to confirm it has good purchase on the stuck round.

Secure the barreled action in a padded bench vise. It is imperative that the gun be held solidly because the tool works on an inertia principle, and if the gun slips in the vise, the force of the slide hammer will be used to pull it free of the vise jaws rather than to pull the live cartridge.

Screw the slide hammer assembly onto the rear of the knurled connector sleeve. As mentioned before, make certain the muzzle is pointed in a safe direction. In addition, do not stand directly behind the gun and the tool. Check to see that the stop nut is screwed tightly to the hammer rod. Standing to the side of the barreled action with the tool attached to the live round, grasp the slide hammer and strike the stop nut sharply.

Continue this operation until the live round is pulled free. After each strike, verify that the collet is still tight on the rim of the cartridge. Inspect the retrieved round and the chamber of the barrel carefully to determine what caused the round to stick and to make sure no barrel obstruction remains. Properly dispose of the pulled round. Do not attempt to salvage it.

Quick-Release Scope Mounts by American Defense (100-003-653WB, $150) use a lever-lock system to clamp an optic onto a flattop rail. The mounts will not work loose, even under heavy recoil.

A large locking bar on the side of the mount engages the maximum amount of rail area, while the cross bolt and two integral locking lugs ensure rock-solid engagement of the rail slots. The more force acting on the lever, the tighter it locks.

The QR lever may be configured to lock to the front or the rear—your preference. Depress the release tab to swing the lever open, and the mount easily lifts off the rifle. Adjustable with a flat-head screwdriver or even a coin,

To secure the optic itself, the hardcoat-anodized aluminum mount uses five heavy-duty steel hex head screws to clamp the vertically split ring halves together. Cutouts in the ring sides and in the base reduce weight without sacrificing strength. Both 1-inch and 30mm rings are available. The entire unit is only 4 ½ inches long and about nine-tenths of an inch tall from the top of the rail to the bottom of the scope body.

the locking lever assures an ultra-secure no-slip fit on almost any Picatinny or Weaver-style rail, including over- or under-sized commercial rails.

Vortex Optics' compact, low-profile **Strikefire Red Dot Scope (100-005-948WB, $170)** fosters fast, both eyes-open sighting with a bright-red or green aiming dot appearing on a wide field of view. It fits MIL-STD 1913 Picatinny rails and Weaver-style bases found on a variety of guns, including flattop AR-15/M16s, tactical shotguns, sporting rifles, and competition pistols.

The Strikefire offers unlimited eye relief through its non-magnifying internal optics and multi-coated lenses. The sight is parallax-free past fifty yards to help you lock onto your target quickly. But if you need it, there's the option of adding the included screw-on 2x magnifier.

Rear-facing rubber-sealed buttons let you control ten steps of brightness and an ultra-low-intensity night vision mode for the 4-minute-of-angle dot, with a separate side control for power on/off. The Strikefire is click-adjustable in ½-MOA increments for windage and elevation, with a 100-MOA maximum range of adjustment. It's compatible with night-vision optics.

The Strikefire is tough, too. The machined-aluminum body is O-ring sealed and nitrogen-purged to be waterproof, fog proof, and shockproof.

The Tactical model has a red aiming dot and an extra-height ring mount to position the scope at the correct height on a flattop AR-15. The Hunter model lets you switch between a red dot and a green dot to set the best color

Both Vortex models run on CR-2 lithium batteries, included, that provide up to 130 hours of red-dot illumination or 420 hours of green dot run time at the maximum brightness setting. The fully coated optics include a 30mm objective lens, but the entire sight is only 6.1 inches long and weighs just 7.2 ounces. In addition to the screw-on 2x magnifier, Vortex supplies flip-up scope covers and instructions with each sight.

The Yankee Hill sight base clamps to Weaver or Picatinny rail systems with a large cross bolt. The knurled and slotted quick-release thumbscrew makes the sight easy to install and remove.

for prevailing light conditions. It comes with a low mount for installation on close-range hunting or tactical rifles.

When a job calls for a compact, strong backup sight system, many tactical shooters choose this **Rear Flip Sight by Yankee Hill Machine (100-002-094WB, $85)**. The steel sight stays locked down out of your sight path until you need it. To deploy the sight, press the spring-loaded pushbutton and it pops up.

While it's on the gun, extra-thick protective ears guard against blows that could bend or break the sight post or aperture. A durable Mil-Spec phosphate coating protects it against the elements. The low-profile design attaches to A4 flattop receivers and regulates correctly with standard, M16/M4 front sights, as well as all Yankee Hill front sights. A large knurled screw head provides half-minute of angle windage adjustment for the flip-style apertures. The .200-inch-diameter peephole offers fast, short-range accuracy. A .065-inch-diameter peephole provides precision for long-range accuracy.

Streamlight makes a host of weapon lights and light/lasers that are suitable for almost any self-defense situation. The **TLR-1s Weapon Lights (100-005-925WB, $130)** are intensely bright, virtually indestructible tactical lights that attach to almost any pistol in seconds. They now feature the latest C4 LED technology, which produces 2 to 3 times the output of previous LEDs. The TLR-1s' high-output C4 LED lamps with impact-resistant Borofloat glass lenses and deep-dish parabolic reflectors produce uniform beams with bright peripheral illumination and no hotspots or shadows. The optics are housed in a machined-aluminum body that

The TLR-1's unique locking-bar system has interchangeable locating keys for secure mounting directly to MIL-STD 1913 Picatinny, Glock-style, S&W 99, S&W TSW, and Beretta 90-Two accessory rails. They fit all holsters designed to accept pistols mounted with the earlier Streamlight M-3, M-5, and M-6 series lights. *Photos this page courtesy of Streamlight.*

On the gun, the TLR-3 light's C4 LED technology projects a high-intensity 90-lumen beam that's two to three times brighter than standard LEDs. An ambi-switch offers momentary or steady-on operation.

Shown here on a Beretta Storm, controls on the TL-4 Weapon Light include an ambidextrous momentary/steady On-Off Switch. A three-position mode-selector switch has settings for laser only, LED illumination only, or both Laser and LED. The TL-4 functions in operating temperatures of –10 °F to +120 °F and is IPX4 rated for water-resistance.

weighs just 4.2 ounces, so the light won't change weapon balance. The TLR-1 produces 135 lumens of continuous light output. The Strobe models, designated with an "s" in the name, produce 160 lumens. The operator can instantly activate the strobe with two rapid taps on the paddle. Both models run on two CR-123 lithium batteries for 2.5 hours of continuous runtime.

The **TLR-3 Compact Weapon Light (100-004-290WB, $75)** is a tiny but powerful illuminator that fits a variety of pistol receiver rails. Weighing only 2.4 ounces—including the provided CF2 lithium battery—the light is only 2 ¾ inches long, 1 ⅛ inches wide, and 1 ½ inches tall from top of the rail clamp to the bottom of the housing. A rail-clamp system allows easy, one-handed attachment or removal from a handgun with MIL-STD 1913 Picatinny rails. It also includes five rail keys to allow installation on certain Berettas, Glocks, Kel-Tecs, Kimbers, and many others.

Streamlight's TL-4 Weapon Light (100-009-757WB, $125) is a high-performance lithium battery–powered flashlight featuring C4 LED Technology and an integrated aiming laser sight. Streamlight's 2.7-inch long C4 LED produces a brighter, more powerful, blinding light than any LED that's come before. The Streamlight-engineered reflector with C4 Photonic Crystal technology creates an intense beam that pierces the darkness without sacrificing the long run times and indestructibility of an LED. The 2.7-ounce rail-mounted light includes a key kit that fits most compact and sub-compact handguns, and the unit also fits most full-sized handguns with rails. The 640–660nm red laser provides targeting in dim or no-light conditions. The windage and elevation adjustment screw is mounted in a brass bushing to ensure the laser's zero holds even during vigorous tactical movement.

LaserLyte's Side Mount Lasers for Ruger's LCP and Kel-Tec's .380 ACP and .32 ACP pistols (100-008-586WB, $85) easily install on these small handguns, providing accurate aiming without adding bulk or weight. The laser with mounting plate weighs only about a quarter ounce and is just over half an inch wide. It's slightly less than four-tenths of an inch thick. The laser mounts on the gun by pushing out and replacing the stock pins with the new screws, which are included.

The side-mounted laser allows the pistol to fit in virtually any nylon pocket holster. To activate, push the laser button with the index finger. During

LaserLyte's SML runs on four No. 377 batteries, which provide 5 hours of constant-on use or 10 hours in pulse mode. The laser can be seen out to 500 yards at night.

the draw, the shooter can use the laser as a finger guide for safe trigger control, without blocking the laser beam. The programmable laser features a pulse or constant-on mode, and it also has an auto-off function to prevent unwanted battery drain.

3Gun Competitions are challenging because the problems presented require creative solutions, such as when a rifle shooter has to engage targets

3GunStuff makes levers for a variety of models, including Trijicon Accupoints, Nightforce Nxs scopes, and Vortex Razor HD scopes. The Scope Lever features an exclusive hinged design with high friction handle. The high friction handle means the lever will always work no matter the conditions. The handle is designed to be the optimum height allowing for plenty of leverage without getting in the way and possibly causing damage by catching on other items.

at different ranges and he needs different scope magnifications. **Scope levers from 3GunStuff (100-007-063WB, $70)** clamp around variable-power zoom rings, providing a convenient way to change magnification settings on the fly.

Most shooters use their weak hand to make the power adjustment with the lever, usually when they're moving between shooting positions with a mix of close and far targets. They'll hold the rifle with the strong hand and zoom or lower the power setting with the other hand, saving valuable time and increasing hits. The scope lever protrudes just enough to push on without becoming an obstruction. The lightweight machined aluminum clamp adds only eight-hundredths of an inch to the outside of the zoom ring, so it won't snag on other gear.

The **RS Products AK 30mm Optics Mount (discontinued)** is a rugged mounting solution for sidemount-equipped Kalashnikov-type rifles. The 30mm Optics Mount is CNC-machined from aircraft-grade 60661-T6 aluminum and weighs only 6 ounces. A steel-locking lever securely clamps the piece to the AK's side mount, keeping its zero if you need to remove the optics. It accepts any optic with a 30mm diameter main tube, such as the Aimpoint M-Series. Once on the gun, the mount puts the optics height at an ideal spot above the AK's dustcover, allowing the optic to be co-witnessed with the iron sights, yet not interfering with field-stripping the AK's action for cleaning. Because AKs vary somewhat in external dimensions, it can be difficult to co-witness the optic and the iron sights using a fixed mount. By

For AK's with stocks that fold to the right side, the RS Products Mount doesn't interfere with locking them in place. However, left-folders will bump into the mount and not lock flat against the receiver. *Photo of the AKM303 mount courtesy RS Products.*

adjusting two hex-head screws in the top, the RS Products Mount allows for nearly a quarter-inch of side-to-side adjustment to ensure the irons and the optics shoot to the same point of impact. Also, the upper half of the mount is punch-marked in case you want to permanently fix the optics location. Adjust the mount to the spot you want it, drill through the punch marks, and insert two supplied pins to fix the location of the mount.

This **Rifle Buttstock Cartridge Carrier by Special Ops Tech (100-004-416WP, $56)** has a built-in pouch that puts 10 rounds of ammunition at the shooter's fingertips. A built-in zippered compartment holds a 10-round tray from a factory ammunition box of .308 Winchester or similarly sized cartridges. An internal, adjustable paracord strap with hook-and-loop fastener cinches the tray snug and keeps it in place for easy shell removal. Of course, cartridges held in the tray stay quiet and in place. The Carrier also provides an integral cheek pad for a comfortable cheek weld. These three adjustable nylon straps with hook-and-loop fasteners and non-slip backing hold the carrier tight on a variety of buttstocks.

The Rifle Buttstock Cartridge Carrier has a rugged Cordura nylon shell in black or coyote brown colors. It fits only right-handed stocks. *Photo courtesy of Special Ops Tech.*

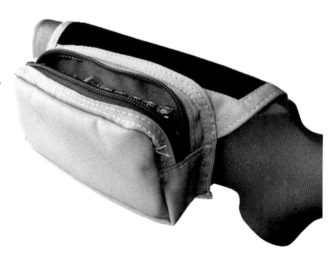

Dallas-based Echo93 specializes in training with and parts for Kalashnikov rifles, including sling-attachment plates for AKM-type stamped-receiver AK-47 and AK-74 rifles and pistols. These **AK Sling Mounts (100-008-778WB, $24)** are made of stamped heavy-duty Parkerized steel and are easy to install. Simply take the AK's grip off, put the Echo Nine Three mount between the grip and receiver, place the grip back into position, then tighten the screw back into place. The ambidextrous Loop V1 fits most stamped-receiver Kalashnikov variants, including both fixed and folding stocks. This includes underfolders, side-folding, and M4-type stocks. The ambi-loop coming off the rear works nicely for either single-point or two-point slings. The loop does not get in the way of the firing hand, and has no sharp edges.

Galco's Miami Classic Shoulder Holster (100-001-634WB, $156) has become the favorite of law enforcement, security and personal-protection professionals because its design allows the user to adjust it for a perfect fit and lasting comfort. Here's the key: All four points of the spider harness can

The Echo Nine Three sling attachments come in several shapes; this one is the reversible V3 loop, which can be used on AKMs as well as right-handed Hungarian-variant AMD-65s and other receivers with a slant-cut rear face.

The V3 also works with some side-folding stocks, depending on the side it folds to, and M4-type stocks. This mount can be used on either side of the receiver, facing either up or down.

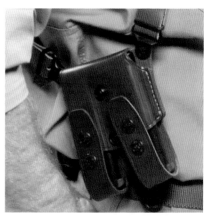

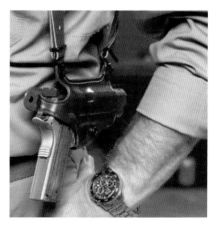

One version of the Galco Miami Classic Shoulder Holster 100-001-634 fits the Beretta Model 92 & 96F/FS semi-autos and the Brigadier pistol, as well as the Taurus PT100/101/92/99 handguns. Another holster secures 1911-style actions, including the AMT Hardballer, Colt, Kimber, Smith & Wesson, and Springfield 1911s and the Star PD pistol. A third style accepts the Glock 17, 19, 22, 23, 26, 27, 31, 32, 33, 34, and 35 models.

pivot independently due to the unique clover-shaped Flexalon swivel back plate. Shooters of all sizes and shapes can tweak each setting until the gun and accessories ride comfortably and are accessible quickly. Made famous when Don Johnson wore it on the television series Miami Vice, this harness is constructed of 1-inch wide premium saddle leather and includes holster, harness, and ammo carrier. The pistol holster is tension-adjustable, and the double magazine carrier has an accessory tab for cuff case or tie down. The leather gets its naturally luminous color from four to six hand-rubbed applications of specially formulated oil. A transparent coating protects the rich burgundy color, repels dirt, and wards off moisture and perspiration.

The **Galco Pocket Protector Holster for Ruger LCR (100-007-584WB, $22)** has a hooked shape that is designed to catch on your pocket—so that you can draw the revolver while the holster remains in your pocket. The

Reinforcements at the holster mouth and beneath the trigger guard keep the Galco Pocket Protector Holster for Ruger LCR 100-007-584 stiff enough to allow a smooth draw and easy return to the holster, while also maintaining enough rigidity to prevent "printing" and shifting of the handgun.

ambidextrous Pocket Protector Holster fits in a front pants pocket or a jacket pocket, keeping the firearm oriented so you can quickly locate the grip when you need to draw. If you're wearing the proper pants or jacket, this premium steerhide holster completely covers and conceals the LCR. Then, if you encounter a non-specific threat, the holster's open-top design allows you to casually place a hand on the butt. If the situation escalates, you have the gun already in hand for the fastest draw.

High Speed Gear's Pistol Taco Pistol Magazine Pouch (100-008-180WB, $25) is a universal pistol-magazine pouch that holds any combination of pistol magazines, including single-stack 1911s, HK45s, the M9/Beretta 92, Glocks, Springfield XDs, and others. The Pistol Taco maintains a positive,

The Pistol Taco by High Speed Gear 100-008-180 can also hold a variety of multi-tools and flashlights securely. It's made in the United States and comes with a MALICE Clip.

adjustable grip on these magazines, and the Taco does not need any other securing system to support it. Made of Cordura nylon, polymer, and shock-cord, the single-mag pouch stays silent when rubbing against the mag body. The fabrics are also quiet when you extract a mag.

Impact Weapons Components Sling Mount-N-Slots (100-006-829WB, $35) allow operators to directly attach slings to firearms and firearm hand guards that have slots and holes, instead of the conventional way of affixing mounts to rail sections. The IWC direct-attach design eliminates the need for a Picatinny rail section and an accompanying quick-detach sling mount. The IWC mounts accept any pushbutton QD sling swivel that connects to any sling system, and the ergonomic design eliminates sharp rail edges that can ensnarl gear. By eliminating the need for a rail, the Impact Weapons Components Mount-N-Slots increase usable Handguard grip area and reduce weight. Micro-Adjustable installation allows the operator to set the mount anywhere through any slot or combination of slots on the firearm Handguard with suitable clearance.

There are several IWC Mount-N-Slot styles. The 100-006-825 unit is the QD Sling Mount-N-Slot, an AR-15 quick-detach sling mount for MOE/ACR hand guards. It accepts heavy-duty or standard 360-degree QD swivels.

The 100-006-826 unit is the QD Rotation-Limited Sling Mount-N-Slot for MOE/ACR hand guards. As its name suggests, it has limited rotation to allow proper positioning of the sling between the firing and carrying position. It prevents sling wrap-up and twist.

The 100-006-827 unit is the Snap Hook Sling Mount-N-Slot for AR-15s with MOE/ACR hand guards. It accepts the HK-style snap hook and Magpul MS2 & MS3 slings. It offers an 8-position mounting capability, and prevents the HK-style hook from accidentally disconnecting.

The Impact Weapons Components Sling Mount-N-Slots are CNC-machined from 6061-T6 aluminum and have a hard-anodized Type III matte finish. Mounting does not require altering the heat shields.

The 100-006-828 model is the OCP Sling Mount-N-Slot for AR-15s, designed for use with MOE/ACR hand guards and Magpul MS2 and MS3 slings. OCP stands for oblique connection point, and the angle of the mount increases attachment speed.

The 100-006-829 model is the TM Snap Hook version for use with MOE carbine, ACR, M4, and A2 hand guards. TM stands for top mount, and it too works with Magpul MS2 & MS3 slings, mounting to the top, or bottom, of the rifle with a snag-decreasing low profile.

The last unit is the 100-006-830 stock number, a top mount HK-style Mount-N-Slot for the AR-15, naturally designed for HK-style slings. For use with MOE carbine, ACR, M4, and A2 hand guards, it too mounts to the top or bottom of the rifle.

Olongapo Outfitters Grab & Go Magazine Pouches (100-004-231WB, $57) are hands-free versions of the metal ammo box. These heavy-duty magazine pouches sling over your shoulder so you can easily carry up to eight fully loaded AR-15 magazines or six UZI-style 9mm stick magazines while on the move. Constructed of woven, water-repelling ballistic nylon that resists tearing and fraying, each compartment has a separate flap, so you won't expose the other mags to the elements when you retrieve one. Generously proportioned Velcro fasteners keep the flaps securely closed, yet release easily when you need a fast reload. The heavy-duty stitching won't give way under stress, and all the exposed edges are protected with tape binding.

The 223/5.56 NATO Olongapo pouches are 12 ½ inches long and 8 inches high. They hold eight 30-round magazines, and the pockets have plenty of length to accommodate magazines fitted with the Magpul Ranger Floorplate. The UZI-style 9mm stick-mag pouches measure 12 ½ inches in length and stand 9 ½ inches tall. Both pouches are available in Coyote Brown and OD Green colors.

Draining grommets in the pockets ensure your mags don't get waterlogged. The 6-foot-long adjustable carry strap, made of 2 inch wide extra-tough nylon webbing, allows you to position the pouch exactly where you need it for fast reloads. Also, the strap's length means that it can be fitted to anyone's torso and should fit over most armor carriers, too. Each of the Grab & Go bags also has a big rear pocket for flat items, such as maps. It is held closed with a 1-inch Velcro strip that runs the entire width of the opening, so anything stored in the rear pocket will be secure.

Built as survival bags for America's elite Special Operations forces and pilots, the **Paladin Go Bag (100-005-433WB, $65)** and **Mission Go Bag (100-005-432WB, $85)** are shaped for smooth extraction and easy access on the run. In extreme environments, Spec Ops shooters use them for escape-and-evasion bags. At home, pack them as emergency bags for the trunk of your car, RV, or boat, or use them as disaster-evacuation overnight bags near the front door of your home. These lightweight bags are made from rugged, rip-resistant nylon material and feature strategically placed and enlarged zipper pulls and buckles that provide easy operation in stressful conditions and bad weather. Reinforced attachment points allow you to pack heavy loads of ammo, survival gear, first-aid supplies, armorer's tools, rations, and

The Go Bag's cylindrical shape makes putting it on and taking it off smooth and easy. It can be worn over the shoulder or in front of the waist. A quick-ditch side-locking buckle and carry handles on each side allow the operator easy access to essential gear.

The versatile Mission Go Bag got its name because of its ability to facilitate numerous missions as a survival go bag, medical bag, explosive breacher bag, sniper bag, tool bag, and laptop bag.

water, and the wide, padded shoulder straps distribute weight comfortably. To keep documents at the ready, a Mission Wallet with eleven small pouches and ID window is included with both bags. With bladders sold separately, their internal hydration reservoirs hold 50 to 100 ounces of water.

The Go Bag's main compartment has double-linked zippers, an internal hydration reservoir slot, four zippered flat-side pockets for small items, three larger zippered external pouches, and attachment webbing on both sides. The internal main zipper is impact-resistant. Externally, it measures 8 inches in width and length and stands 20 inches tall. The coyote-brown-colored bag weighs 2 pounds.

The Mission Go Bag is equipped with a large zippered main compartment and a bellowed zippered front pocket. The main compartment has four draw-cord 500 mL IV pouches, a flat-items pouch, and a sewn-in tape dispenser. The Mission Go Bag allows five methods of carry: padded shoulder strap, waist pack, briefcase, MOLLE vest mount, and wall mount. With optional equipment, it can also be toted as a belt mount, chest mount, pack lid, backpack, or stowed in a Mission Pack. It can go from shouldered bag to a waist or fanny pack with a fold and snap. As a briefcase, it is designed to carry military-issue Panasonic Toughbooks and other laptops of similar size. Made of 1000-denier nylon, it weighs 2 ½ pounds and is 4 ½ inches thick, 11 ½ inches long, and 10 ¼ inches tall.

Seahorse Pistol Cases (100-005-943WB, $120) have high-impact polypropylene shells that can withstand heavy abuse in any environment. Inside, high-density Accuform foam padding secures pistols in pre-cut slots or customizable blocks. Each case is sealed with a rubber O-ring, which is captured in a tongue-and-groove channel in the lid. When the lid snaps shut, the seal keeps out water and dust. Also built into the black shell is an automatic pressure-relief system for easy opening after air travel. Sturdy ridges protect hinges, easy-opening latches, and molded-in padlock holes. These cases meet TSA checked-baggage guidelines, along with other stringent standards for military use and theft protection.

The SE-540FP4 (100-005-943WB) and SE-540F (100-005-944WB, $92) are large boxes that weigh about 6 ½ pounds unloaded. They measure 15 inches long, just over 12 inches wide, and 9 ½ inches tall. Internal storage area is 13 ½ inches long, 9 ¾ inches wide, and 8 ⅜ inches high.

Inside the Seahorse SE-540FP4, die-cut foam holds four downward-facing handguns, eight magazines, and two revolver speed loaders.

A large cavity has room for a box of ammo or other items.

The SE-540F has a full foam insert the owner can custom-cut to his needs.

The SE-300F features a customizable pick foam insert in the foam to hold a single revolver or 1911-size semi-auto, plus two magazines and a box of ammunition.

The SE-300F's (100-005-945WB) exterior measures 10 ¾ inches long, 10 inches wide, and 4 ½ inches high. Internally, it provides a carry space that's 9 ½ inches long, 7 ½ inches wide, and 4 inches high. It weighs 2.8 pounds unloaded.

This is T.H.E. Pack. It's not just a pack; it's T.H.E. Pack, which stands for Tactical Holds Everything Pack. Made from tough Cordura nylon in black or coyote brown colors, this **Spec.-Ops. T.H.E.Pack (100-005-967WB, $160)** really does hold nearly everything. On the outside it stands 19 inches high, 13 inches wide, and is 12 inches deep at bottom, tapering to 9 inches at the top. It presents 2550 cubic inches of storage space.

T.H.E. Pack, which weighs 3.6 pounds empty, is compatible with the Spec.-Ops. X-System magazine, cargo, and utility pouches.

The contrasting bright-yellow lining helps you find items in dim light.

On the inside, a roomy main compartment—19 inches high, 13 inches wide and 7 inches deep—features a zippered mesh pocket and a pocket for a hydration bag or radio. Left and right openings with hook-and-loop closures provide external routing for a water tube, antenna, or microphone cord. Elsewhere, three compartments have fast-opening, #10 YKK zippers for instant access to essential items. Trademarked GRIDLOCK loops on each pocket face, as well as the sides and bottom of the main compartment, let you configure accessories or attach extra storage pouches.

Dual expansion straps let you cinch the bag tight to the load to keep it quiet and compact. Padded shoulder straps have built-in loops for attaching additional accessories. An adjustable chest strap can be repositioned or removed entirely. If needed, the 2-inch waist strap can be removed to use the bag as a shoulder pack. In this orientation, the double-layer pack top prevents stress failure caused by heavy use of carry handle.

The **Shotgun AR-15 Stock Conversion by Cavalry Mfg. (100-001-456WB, $310)** is a machined-aluminum stock adapter with Picatinny rail lets you install an AR-15 or M4 buttstock on your Remington 870 or Mossberg 500 or 590 pump gun. It uses any AR-15–style stock and grip, providing the familiar handling qualities of an AR-15. Of course, the conversion provides easier cross training for shooters who use AR-15s or M16 rifles. The Stock Conversion adapter was specifically designed to provide a proper cheek weld when the shooter is using optics on the shotgun.

Optics can be mounted on the Conversion's Picatinny rail, which duplicates the dimensions of a flattop AR-15 upper receiver. Because the rail is the same height, the shooter sees a sight picture like that of an optic mounted on an AR-15. Also, putting the stock inline with the bore reduces felt recoil.

Cavalry's standard Conversion Unit includes the adapter and rail assembly only, which accepts your receiver extension tube, buttstock, and pistol grip. The M4 system includes a collapsible stock and pistol grip.

The **Brownells Basic Shotgun Cleaning Kit (084-000-335WB, $46)** is a handy, money-saving package filled with top-quality cleaning products for your 12-gauge shotgun. If you purchased these items separately, you'd spend right at $90. Just add a good cleaning rod, and you're fully equipped to maintain your 12-gauge shotgun in top form. The Kit includes a 4-ounce bottle of Brownells Shotgun Wad Solvent, three hard-scrubbing Double-Tuff bronze bore brushes, three absorbent cotton-fiber bore mops, and 200 cotton-flannel patches. You also get a 4-ounce bottle of corrosion-inhibiting Friction Defense Gun Oil, 24 ounces of TCE aerosol cleaner/degreaser, a handy, double-ended small parts brush, and a large, absorbent cotton shop cloth for a thorough wipe down at the end. All this is tucked into the case's huge 13 ¼ by 6 ¾ by 5-¼-inch storage section. There's also an integral small-parts compartment accessible without opening up the rest of the box.

The deluxe hard-plastic case has a hinged lid and a comfortable fold-down carry handle. When you're ready to pack the Shotgun Cleaning Kit up, a hefty cam latch pulls the cover down tight, while a rubber gasket forms a watertight seal.

I've had several Mossberg Model 500 pump shotguns, and a niggling issue I don't like about the gun is the polymer safety slider. When the gun is wet or I'm wearing gloves, my thumb can sometimes slip over the safety tab. Fixing the safety is probably the most common repair on Mossberg's 500-series shotguns, which are otherwise tank-simple and durable. The location of the safety is ideal, but I don't like the design. The plastic safety button on some 500 models can break, and the safety button is held in place by a single short screw, which can work loose.

The Mossberg 500/590/835 Enhanced
Safety Button 080-000-539WB features
all-steel construction for durability and a
higher profile for improved handling.

The plastic safety button on some
500 models, such as this Mariner,
can break.

If the screw does loosen, the safety button and other parts can drop out and turn the gun into nothing more than a glorified club. The **Mossberg 500/590/835 Enhanced Safety Button (080-000-539WB, $20)** is a direct replacement for the factory button that features all-steel construction for durability and a higher profile for improved handling. The raised ridges in the replacement button give my thumb more surface to push and pull on, offering fast, sure operation on the first try.

One of the hidden benefits built into the button is its reversible shape. I have short thumbs, so I place the raised pad toward the rear, making the safety easier for me to reach. Shooters with longer thumbs may prefer the pad located farther forward.

Replacing the factory safety also gives me a chance to replace the factory safety button screw at the same time. The screw that Mossberg uses is a one-way screw—half of each side of the slot is rounded. This allows you to tighten it, but you can't loosen it very easily. The screw that's provided in the **Brownells Mossberg 500/590/835 Safety Kit (080-000-564WB, $40)** is also this one-way type.

When I put the new safety button on, I prefer to affix it with a blued #6-32 Fillister Head screw. Fillister Head screws are machine-thread types used in a pre-tapped hole with or without a nut. The Fillister Head has a rounded top surface, cylindrical sides, and a flat bearing surface. The greater side height is what distinguishes it from a Pan Head. It is the preferred head style for use in counterbored holes.

Brownells sells 12-paks of #6-32s (#080-050-632WB) for $6. In the past, I've used a hacksaw to cut the 1-inch-long screw to about ⅜ inch length, then Dremel-ground it to the approximate 5⁄16-inch final length. I find the perfect length by grinding the screw then running the piece in, until it fits flush. Then I cold-blue the exposed tip, and blue Loc-Tite it in place. If you don't want to mess with all that, you may also be able to find the right screw dimensions online and buy the smallest possible quantity. However, such screws may not be as hard as Brownells' pieces, so caveat emptor.

Tip: I would be remiss if I didn't point out that installing this seemingly simple part is not just a drop-in task. It requires disassembling the action and removing the trigger. Detailed instructions are included when you buy either the Enhanced Safety Button alone or the Safety Kit—and nothing in the process is especially difficult—but the job is more than popping a new safety tab on.

More and more firearms are receiving sprayed-on finishes, which offer the triple benefits of sealing underlying steel or wood from corrosion, allowing a lot of colors and patterns, and spraying on fast and easy. An easy-to-use product for that is **Lauer Custom Weaponry's DuraCoat Shake 'N Spray Finishing Kit (100-006-802WB, $30)**. DuraCoat is a two-part chemical coating. Unlike other firearm finishes, DuraCoat was created specifically for firearms.

DuraCoat is dry to the touch in 20 minutes, can be handled in 1 hour, and is ready for use overnight. DuraCoat will gain most of its final hardness, elasticity and chemical resistance over a 2- to 3-week period. To apply to wood, degrease and lightly sand wood surfaces, then apply DuraCoat. Allow to dry overnight.

In the case of firearm finishes, a common misconception is "harder is better." Hardness means brittle, and brittle means chipping. DuraCoat, being elastic, will not chip. If your DuraCoat chips, it means you have a preparation problem. Most likely, the surface was not clean. Elasticity provides protection by giving when confronted with impact. Elasticity also helps prevent scratches and mars.

With normal use, a firearm finished with DuraCoat will last several lifetimes. DuraCoat loves hard-coat anodizing and Parkerizing as a base. Both processes leave a good rooting surface for DuraCoat. DuraCoat can withstand temperatures as high has 500–600 °F. With "normal" shooting, your barrel will never get close to being that hot. The Shake 'N Spray Finishing Kit contains 10 milliliters of DuraCoat hardener, 6 ounces of TruStrip cleaner/degreaser, 4 ounces of DuraCoat matte black coating, a scrubbing pad, an aerosol sprayer with a jar, and instructions. DuraCoat was designed for the average gun owner. Preheating, baking, and blasting are not required. Simply clean and degrease the surface prior to application.

To use the Shake 'N Spray Finishing Kit, first degrease metal parts with the enclosed TruStrip cleaner and pad. Some degreasers, especially those used in the automotive industry, can leave a residue. This residue will form a barrier between the surface and DuraCoat, causing a coating failure. TruStrip cleans the contaminates commonly found on and in firearms and will not leave a residue. Then mix the DuraCoat in the provided jar, and spray the finish on. Hang the parts to let them dry.

Brownells Triple Tough Premium Storage Bags (083-054-003WB, $10) are intended for extreme long-term storage under changing conditions of heat and humidity. When properly sealed, these Storage Bags are impervious to water in either vapor or liquid form, and are highly resistant to common gun solvents, oils, preservative oils and greases. They are resistant to tears or puncturing, either from parts stored or outside influences, and are heat resistant for storage up to about 160 °F.

Tough but flexible, these bags are puncture resistant, semi-transparent and have a 0 percent moisture transmission rating, so rust-protected items sealed inside will remain rust and corrosion free indefinitely. They are resistant to all petroleum-based chemicals and solvents and are completely non-biodegradable, so they will never break down, even in full contact with soil or moisture. Also, anti-static properties make them a perfect dust cover for short-term storage in a vault, or even in the back corner of a closet.

To use the bags, make certain that all firearms placed into storage are empty and unloaded; personally verify that the chamber, magazine, and cartridge feeding devices do not contain ammunition. Gun box labels are provided to properly identify the gun preserved in the storage bag. Be sure to add the date of storage on the label.

Important: The exterior section of the Storage Bag should be on a flat surface when the tape is applied, and the tape should be applied in a smooth, continuous strip of at least two full wraps around the sealed end of the bag.

Firearms placed into long-term storage should be completely cleaned and properly lubricated with a non-gumming lubricant. Pay special attention to the bore. Thoroughly clean the bore and make certain there is no jacket or lead fouling left in the bore prior to storage. Jacket or lead fouling may corrode with oxygen present in the storage bag and damage the bore.

If preservative oils or greases are used on the firearm, disassemble to the point that the stock(s) can be removed, and coat the metal parts with the preservative oil/grease following the manufacturer's instructions. Carefully wrap the wood parts in butcher paper (available at your local grocery store) or unused newsprint paper. Place all parts to be stored into the bag, and squeeze out as much air as possible. Fold the open end over three times with at least a 1-inch folded section on each fold. Seal the folded section with polyethylene tape, going completely around the bag.

An easier alternative is to use **Brownells Rust-Blox Vapor Tabs (083-000-001)** or **Brownells Gunwrap Paper (084-031-010)** to chemically prevent any oxygen remaining in the bag from reacting with the metal parts to form oxides (rust). No disassembly is required with this method, and guns can be returned to service much quicker than would be possible if preservative oils or greases are used. Both products are dated and must be changed at intervals to assure continued corrosion protection.

The Storage Bag can be heat-sealed as an alternative to tape. Use a regular clothes iron, with the heat setting just hot enough that you can visibly see the bag fuse. Do not fold the bag when heat-sealing; it should be laid perfectly flat, with all excess air squeezed out. Use just the edge of the iron, and start fusing the bag on the outer, open end of the bag, fusing in several strips to ensure a full seal.

To open the storage bag after heat-sealing, use sharp scissors or a sharp knife. The bag may be re-sealed if either a shorter gun is to be stored or the initially sealed area is far enough from the end of the gun that you have enough room to get a good seal the second time around. Make sure there is no dirt, grease or oil in the area to be fused.

The bolt on your Remington Model 700 was not designed to be field-stripped by the shooter, but **Sinclair's Bolt Maintenance Kit (749-011-311WB, $116)** makes it easy to completely disassemble your Model 700 bolt for cleaning or replacement of components. The Sinclair kit contains a

This case features storage for the Remington Firing Pin Removal Tool (RFPT), Remington Ejector Compressor Tool, Remington Mainspring Tool, and Remington Bolt Maintenance Bench Block.

Remington firing pin removal tool, a mainspring-changing tool, and an ejector compressor tool, along with a bench block that holds your bolt steady while you work on it.

Bolt disassembly begins with the Sinclair Firing Pin Tool, which retracts the cocking piece far enough to clear a detent, allowing you to unscrew the bolt shroud/firing pin assembly from the bolt body. The Mainspring Tool then compresses the mainspring until a retaining pin on the cocking piece is exposed. You knock out the retaining pin with a punch, and then gradually release Mainspring Tool pressure until the mainspring is relaxed. You can now remove the shroud and mainspring.

Replacing or repairing the Remington plunger ejector is even easier. Simply push the bolt through the open end of the "C"-shaped Ejector Tool, then rotate it 90 degrees so the locking lugs hold it in place. This allows you to remove the ejector retainer pin and remove the ejector and its spring. Your Model 700 bolt is now completely disassembled.

After cleaning, lubricating and/or replacing components, you can reassemble the bolt by simply reversing the takedown procedure. The Sinclair Remington Bolt Maintenance Kit comes with a sturdy, fitted case for convenient storage.

Kimber's Rimfire Target Conversion Kit (387-000-045WB, $320) turns your full-size 45 into an economical 22 Long Rifle training handgun in minutes. Simply remove the factory slide and barrel, replace them with the conversion unit, and load the included 22 Long Rifle magazine with premium-grade high-velocity ammunition.

The blowback-operated sub-caliber conversion unit lets you shoot less expensive 22 ammunition in any Mil-Spec 1911 Government model. The Kimber Kit preserves the full-bore pistol's weight, balance, and overall feel to help you develop specific skills and muscle memory to shoot better with full-power ammo.

The Conversion Kit components are manufactured to the same rigorous quality standards as Kimber's full-power 1911 pistols. The slide is precision machined from aluminum billet, has wide front and rear cocking serrations, and wears Kimber's tough, scratch-resistant, KimPro II finish. The Kit fits 1911 Government model pistols chambered in 45 ACP with 4- or 5-inch non-ramped barrels and dimensional tolerances that meet US Government specs, including Series 70 and 80 Colt pistols and clones.

The Kimber's aluminum slide, finished in matte black or silver, does not lock open after last shot. The pistol may be dry-fired with the kit installed, and it requires high-velocity ammunition for proper operation.

The Kit comes with plain black target sights installed, and the rear sight is click adjustable for windage and elevation. The flat, finely serrated rear face creates a non-reflective surface that makes the rear square notch read crisp and clean. It includes a ramped match-grade 5-inch stainless barrel with a 1-in-16-inch left-hand twist and stainless steel match-grade bushing. Its reinforced polymer 10-round magazine is designed for a secure fit in a standard 45 ACP mag well, and has an anti-tilt polymer follower to ensure smooth feeding of rounds.

The **Ghost 3.5 Trigger Control Connector (100-000-936, $9)** is a stainless-steel tab internally fitted on your Glock that shortens and lightens your pistol's trigger response. The easy-to-install drop-in connector lowers a Glock's trigger-pull weight to 3.5 pounds for competition and sporting use. There are no screws to come loose and jam your gun, and you do not have to buy a trigger housing. The Ghost 3.5 tabs come factory polished, resulting in the smoothest possible contact surfaces and a consistent trigger pull every time. According to Ghost, no other process, including plating, produces less friction between contact points on your trigger.

The Ghost 3.5 Trigger Control Connector is also self-cleaning. Channels in the tab prevent debris from building up on the trigger mechanism surfaces, causing additional friction.

Many shooters feel the standard Glock magazine release is too short and the extended Glock release is too long. In addition, both versions have sharp edges. The **Vickers Extended Glock Magazine Release by TangoDown (100-003-404, $17)** is a slightly extended magazine release for the Glock series of 9mm, 40 S&W, and 357 SIG pistols and now the Glock 20, 21, 29, and 30 series of pistols. A collaborative effort between competitive shooter and tactician Larry Vickers and TangoDown, the black-plastic magazine release is molded from the same material as the factory original but is slightly extended and has rounded edges.

The **Tactical Supply Depot Magazine Baseplates with Custom Logos (100-006-022WB, $25)** puts a little bit of personality on your semiauto

The Vickers extended magazine release is easy to find and operate, allowing fast, smooth mag changes that save you precious seconds. The serrated release button is ³/₃₂-inch longer than original, allowing easy thumb access without repositioning your hand. It replaces the factory original without alteration in Glock Models 17, 19, 22 through 24, 26 and 27, and 31 through 35.

The Tactical Supply Depot Magazine Baseplates etchings appear as light grey colors. The baseplates slide on and off the magazine body just like a factory plate, making them easy to remove for cleaning.

pistol. These customized replacements for factory plastic baseplates are precision machined from lightweight, durable aluminum and laser-etched with a custom logo that gives your pistol a unique touch. The plates come etched with a patriotic American Flag, an aggressive death's head Punisher, the international Biohazard sign, or a Happy Face logo. They'll fit Smith & Wesson M&Ps, Springfield XDs, Springfield XD-Ms, and Glocks.

Also, plain baseplates without any logo are available for Glocks only. Please note that the Glock plates are machined to extremely close tolerances and require minor fitting. Instructions on how to do that are included. The Tactical Supply Magazine Baseplates with Custom Logos are made of 6061 T6 aluminum, are hardcoat anodized, and come with a matte-black background color.

Chip McCormick Custom's 1911 Auto 10-Round Power Magazines (207-000-025, $35) are extra-heavy-duty units designed to increase reliability and service life, even when the mag is kept fully loaded and seated in a pistol for extended periods. The mag's feed lips are roll-formed and polished, not die cut, for added strength, and Chip's follower design provides flawless feeding with semi-wadcutters and hollow points. Inside, a powerful spring of proprietary heat-treated Rocket Wire further ensures reliable feeding. A removable plastic base pad with full front-to-back engagement is built to withstand continual use, and numbered witness holes on both sides of the body provide a fast, visible round count.

The Chip McCormick long-body 10-round model has a base pad that wraps around the exposed portion of magazine that extends beyond the mag well. Power Plus models have an advanced anti-tilt follower for even better support of the round stack.

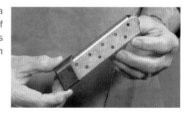

Jerry Miculek is the fastest revolver shooter alive, and he's designed these **S&W Miculek Competition Grips (100-000-219WB, $70)** to allow speed shooters a fast draw and maximum recoil control. The smooth, narrow design features an open backstrap for a comfortable grip and excellent trigger reach. The Pau Ferro wood grip isn't checkered, so clothing slides over it easily. Several Brownells customers commented on how much they like the Miculek Competition Grips. Marc, an LE/Military shooter from Saint Joseph, Illinois, gave his grip a perfect 5.0 rating and said it added "a touch of functional class!" He said, "I put a set on my 327-R8. It's amazing how they reposition your hand and put your grip in a natural point of aim. I am buying another set for my 629."

The Miculek Competition Grip's one-piece design provides a solid fit to the frame, for sure steering from target to target.

S&W Junkie, a gun collector from the San Francisco Bay Area, said, "These feel great in your hand. They really lend a feeling of complete command and control of the handgun. The metal-to-wood fit is like a glove—literally, it's that precise and snug."

These **Extended Basepads & Springs for Glock Pistols (100-002-221WB, $33)** slide onto your existing 40 S&W and 9mm magazines, increasing capacity by up to four rounds. Made by Dawson Precision, the aluminum base pads add three rounds to the capacity of 15-round 40 S&W Glock magazines. The 9mm base pads add four more rounds to your small-frame Glock magazines. They're also easy to install, requiring no special tools. The base pads slip onto the magazine bodies and lock into place. They're just as easy to remove for cleaning. Each set comes with an extra-power steel spring and installation instructions.

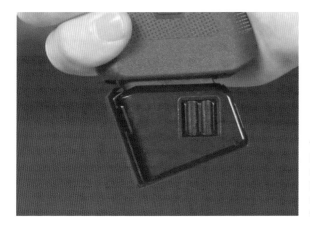

The Dawson Extended Basepads fit under the 140mm USPSA magazine-length rule. They are a must-have for any competitive Glock shooter.

Gunsmiths and hobbyists love the precise, pre-fit dimensions on the **1911 Auto Drop-In Match Barrels by Ed Brown (087-925-450WB, $180).** The Brown barrels' slightly oversized dimensions create tighter barrel lockup for match-quality accuracy with little or no fitting needed. Using the most modern CNC machinery and manufacturing methods, Ed Brown craftsmen manufacture barrels in house. The barrels are made from a 3-pound chunk of T-416 gun-barrel-quality stainless steel bar stock, which is stress-relieved

The complete barrel kit includes pre-fit, match-grade barrel, bushing, link, and pin for faster installation in 4.25-inch Commander lengths and 5-inch Government Model lengths.

and heat-treated prior to final rifling and refinishing. According to Ed Brown, they're rifled by precision broach in the original configuration designed by John Browning: six lands and grooves, one turn in sixteen, left-hand twist. This deep-cut, broached rifling gives superior accuracy with all types of bullets, including lead.

Aimpoint Micro-series sights are small, light, and rugged red-dot sights developed for hunting, sport shooting, military, and law-enforcement applications. The **Aimpoint Micro H-1 (100-003-004WB, $588)** was designed with the hunter in mind. It is Aimpoint's lightest red-dot sight and is easy to carry and fast to aim. It is small enough to be used on a lightweight rifle, a hunting revolver, a shotgun, or even a bow, and it is unaffected by extreme weather. The H-1 Micro has a bright, glowing 4-minute red dot with twelve daylight settings and one extra-bright setting. Using the integral Weaver-style base, it attaches easily to most firearms. The parallax-free H-1 Micro allows you to shoot accurately in low light and with both eyes open, which speeds target acquisition. The dot follows the movement of the shooter's eye while remaining fixed on the target, and it allows for unlimited eye relief.

The sight's exclusive Advanced Circuit Efficiency Technology, or ACET, greatly improves the useable life of the single CR2032 lithium battery.

The matte-black H-1 measures less than 2½ inches in length and width and is only 1.6 inches tall. With the mount, it weighs only 3.7 ounces.

The H-1 Micro sight can last nearly 50,000 hours of constant use—or more than five years—at position 8 of 12.

A proprietary housing and lens-sealing material keeps the H-1's electronic and lens surfaces dry, fog-free, and fully functional regardless of weather conditions. The 1-power sight is adjustable for windage and elevation, and the adjustment tool is built into the knob caps for convenience.

The **Fastfire Red Dot Reflex Sight by Burris (118-000-019WB, $230)** is a compact red-dot sight that provides fast, accurate, both-eyes-open sighting on handguns, rifles, and tactical shotguns. A high-intensity LED projects a 4-MOA red sighting dot on the heads-up display, while a light sensor and integrated control circuitry adjust the dot's brightness to match the light around the target. The sight's coated, dual-layer lens resists scratches and scuffs and is parallax-free to 50 yards.

Looking through the sight, you can see how the mild 1.07-power magnification helps you acquire long-range targets, without compromising close-in effectiveness. Setting the point-of-impact is easy and secure with two flush-mounted screws that provide 190 inches of windage and elevation adjustments at 100 yards. A low-profile control switch resists accidental activation and has positive clicks for On and Off positions.

All this functionality would be worthless if the FastFire II weren't stout. The robust stainless steel and aluminum housing can handle the recoil of

So that your FastFire II is ready to roll when you receive it, it comes with one 3-volt CR 2032 lithium battery, which will last up to five years when the sight is used in Battery Saver mode. Also included are a snap-on cover, a windage and elevation scale disc and adjustment tool, and instructions.

magnum shotgun loads. Also, it will continue to function even after being submerged. A bottom plate gasket seals it against water intrusion.

Most shooters will prefer to get the sight with a base that mounts to MIL-STD 1913 Picatinny and Weaver-style rails. Or the sight is available separately (118-000-020WB, $199) and fits mounts that accept the original FastFire sight. Installed, it weighs less than 2 ounces.

Making accurate long-range shots is now easier than ever, thanks to the speed and simplicity of these laser range-finding riflescopes from Nikon, the **AR-15/M16 M-223 Laser IRT models (100-009-880WB, from $450)**. The Nikon M-223 Laser IRT, short for Immediate Range Technology, removes the guesswork from proper shot placement and saves you precious seconds switching from a handheld rangefinder to the riflescope. The M-223 riflescope provides laser-ranging information within the scope. Activate the laser with a one-touch button and instantly see the distance results displayed.

Then use the open-circle aiming points and hash marks in the BDC 600 Reticle to place an accurate shot from 100 to 600 yards. The bullet-drop compensating reticles are calibrated for the .223 Remington/5.56 NATO round, specifically 55-grain polymer-tipped bullets travelling at 3240 feet per second. Other shooter enhancements include zero-reset turrets that simplify

The Nikon M-223 Laser IRT is nitrogen filled and O-ring sealed to make it waterproof, fog proof, and shockproof.

field adjustments, a low-profile built-in mounting system, and smooth zooming from 2.5- to 10-power magnification.

Multi-Function LED Flashlights made by Inforce-Mil (100-006-191WB, $220) are built for hard use. Their carbon-fiber-reinforced polymer bodies are lightweight, yet the shells stand up to hard impact and shock. Also, the flashlights use powerful light-emitting diodes instead of traditional incandescent bulbs, which can fail due to shock or impact.

Both plain white and white-plus-color models are available in the in ultra-compact 6-volt and 9-volt lights. In the entire line, solid-state circuitry and power management ensure the longest possible run times, so these lights won't leave you in the dark at the wrong moment.

One plain-white 6-volt model and one plain-white 9-volt unit offer three-mode tailcap switches with Momentary, Constant-On, and Lockout, or Off, settings. The 6VX and 9VX plain white models have five lighting modes: Momentary, High Constant, Low Constant, CQB Strobe, and Lockout.

The 6V and 6VX models are 4 ¾ inches long, measure 1 inch in diameter, and weigh only 3.3 ounces when loaded with two CR-123 lithium batteries, which are included. The 9V and 9VX are 6 inches long and 1 ¼ inches in diameter. They weigh just 4 ¾ ounces when loaded with three provided CR-123 lithium batteries.

The Color models feature a powerful white main LED illuminator with low-, medium-, and high-output levels, plus secondary colors. Those secondary colors are low-power white, red to preserve night vision, green for map reading in vehicles, and blue for detection of dried fluids. The Color units are also available with an Infrared emitter instead of a low-power white LED.

The Color LE Strobing model offers red, blue, and white secondary LEDs. The slow-strobing mode can serve as an individual marker. The high-speed-strobe setting can be used to disorient attackers. The Color Series lights are 6 ¼ inches long and 1 ¼ inches in diameter. They weigh 4 ½ ounces, including two supplied CR-123 lithium batteries.

Their O-ring-sealed bodies have ultra-sonic welded components, and the rubber-sealed tailcap switches are waterproof to 66 feet. All of the lights employ a one-way venting system. That lets heat out to prevent overheating during extended operation. All models come with a detachable stainless-steel belt clip, and are available in black or desert sand colors.

All of these lights can be converted to weapon lights using the Inforce Flashlight Rail Mount and Remote Pressure Switch, both available separately. Mounted like that, shooters will appreciate the lights' intuitive tailcap switches, which allow one-handed operation, including changing the mode.